NOT GOD'S TYPE

HOLLY ORDWAY

NOT GOD'S TYPE

An Atheist Academic
Lays Down Her Arms

Foreword by
John Mark N. Reynolds

IGNATIUS PRESS   SAN FRANCISCO

To Jim and Kathy Ordway

Fallen man is not simply an imperfect creature who needs improvement: he is a rebel who must lay down his arms.

—C. S. Lewis

[The Prodigal Son] must *surrender himself* to his lawful Sovereign. He is a runaway offender; he must come back, as a very first step, before anything can be determined about him, bad or good; he is a rebel, and must lay down his arms.

—Blessed John Henry Cardinal Newman

St Michael and All Angels

Michaelmas gales assail the waning year,
And Michael's scale is true, his blade is bright.
He strips dead leaves, and leaves the living clear
To flourish in the touch and reach of light.
Archangel bring your balance, help me turn
Upon this turning world with you and dance
In the Great Dance. Draw near, help me discern,
And trace the hidden grace in change and chance.
Angel of fire, Love's fierce radiance,
Drive through the deep until the steep waves part;
Undo the dragon's sinuous influence
And pierce the clotted darkness in my heart.
Unchain the child you find there, break the spell
And overthrow the tyrannies of Hell.

—Malcolm Guite

This poem has been used by the kind permission of its author; it is from *Sounding the Seasons: Seventy Sonnets for the Christian Year* (London: Canterbury Press, 2012).

CONTENTS

FOREWORD

Intellectuals have given themselves a bad name. Often they seem cut off from the 'real world' or the values that exalt a nation. But there have been and are a few thoughtful people, intellectuals in the positive sense, who love ideas and people.

When I was a young man, the story of C. S. Lewis, the atheist literature professor turned Christian, inspired me to an academic life and now as a university administrator the story of another atheist professor trained in literature who turned to Jesus Christ as an adult motivates me to keep going and to do better than I have done.

Ordway is a new kind of apologist. If Francis Schaeffer pioneered a type of cultural apologetics that our colleague Nancy Pearcey is bringing to maturity, then Ordway is providing a new starting place incarnating a compatible, but unique vision of what it means to be an apologist and a scholar today.

Following twentieth-century examples such as Dietrich Bonhoeffer, Ordway is unafraid of culture and reminds us that we live in the world, even if we are not of the world. We have bodies and souls, souls and bodies, and Ordway's apologetic never forgets either one or puts the emphasis on any question in the wrong place.

Some have worshipped creation or used 'creation care' as a slogan for functional materialism. Others use a theology of the body as a start at loosening Christian morals. We have too many Christian academics, Christian intellectuals, and Christian artists for whom Christianity is merely a modifying adjective to the substance of their lives or careers. Ordway is a rarity: a Christian who does things, an academic Christian, an intellectual Christian, and an artistic Christian.

This book shows that the linguistic shift matters.

She accepts the full gospel, not because she always likes it, but because she thinks it the best, truest, and most beautiful idea in human history. Ordway is hardheaded enough to accept the failures of Christians and will not defend our schisms, genocides, or decadence.

She never loses sight of Jesus: incarnate, triumphant, and alive.

I know she is God's type, but she is not always any type the twenty-first century can handle. She is smart, powerful, feminine, and traditional. Her views are unpredictable, because she forms them on the Word of God.

Some smart folk wish to love Jesus, but prefer to ignore his bride, the Church. This goes no better for these rude people than it does when any loving husband meets a boor who condescends, ignores, or insults his beloved. Ordway loves the people of God, because she loves God. This does not blind her to some of the problems of the visible Church, but her reasoning does not end with easy cynicism.

Ordway's story is the story of God planting his word within her, Ordway (eventually!) responding, "Let it be done unto me", and then finding her way to an ecclesiastical home. She thinks for herself, but not by herself. She looks for the mind of Christ and the community of faith in all ages.

If I do not share all her conclusions about the nature of the Church, I do share her knowledge that the Church is both visible and invisible. She is not a creature of institutions, but of the Incarnation. She knows that just as men must have bodies to be men, so the bride of Christ must be visible to be a bride of an incarnate Christ.

At the same time, the Church is mystical and fully seen only in paradise. Ordway knows how to reason (ask her students), but she is not afraid to stop and worship when she reaches the ineffable. She has a sense that beauty can be a snare, but it can also be a sign.

Ordway's story is one in which fear is replaced by love. God does not fear questions, doubts, worries, or mistakes. He fears nothing, because he is perfect love. Ordway sensed this truth even when she was distant from God and so exchanged her fears and self-doubt for love.

She found a Person, but in finding him also found his family: the Church. She is not so arrogant as to demand that the family live up to her expectations, even when those expectations are justified!

Should a person whom we hope is merely in the middle of her story tell it? If pride was the motivation or self-indulgence, then no Christian could justify a memoir, but this book is in the tradition of the testimony. As a young boy, I loved hearing the saints-in-process of all ages share what Jesus was doing in their lives. Such stories encourage believers to carry on. We know the Church will endure, but we wobble.

The gates of hell will not prevail against the Church, but they often feel like they are crushing me. At that moment the testimony of a believer about the state of her walk with God is most encouraging. Dr. Ordway is a joyful warrior, a status that implies not just good cheer, something she surely has, but a willingness to fight.

I know many culture warriors, but few jolly culture warriors: Holly Ordway is one.

If I had the power, I would declare Dr. Ordway a 'shield maid of Rohan'. If you understand the reference and enjoy it, then you are the kind of student Dr. Ordway inspires every day here at HBU. Like Lewis, Tolkien, or Sayers, Ordway is imaginative and full of living faith, but unlike them she is American. She is a child of her nation, though not in some narrow or jingoistic sense.

Ordway grew up experiencing American culture and American Christianity in the last few decades. She watched American television, listened to American music, and attended very good American schools. An early and lazy secularism mutated into a more militant atheism in that environment, but she eventually had the chance to meet serious Christians. If Americans have a single national virtue, it must be hope.

Now she is the first chair of a cultural apologetics program at Houston Baptist University. Is there anything more American, more hopeful, than that?

Now reading her life reflections, we get to peek into the life of an intellectual warrior, Christian, and scholar.

John Mark N. Reynolds
Feast of the Martyred Tsar, 2013
Houston Baptist University

Preface

I wrote the first version of this book just two years into my Christian journey, noting that as time went on, I would surely see more than I did at the time of writing, and that, as I continued to reflect, the story would gradually become clearer. Indeed, this has turned out to be the case.

Following the first publication of *Not God's Type*, I gave many interviews and presentations on "an atheist's journey to faith", and was asked perceptive questions: What was my childhood experience of faith? How did I become an atheist in the first place? What changed so that I became willing to listen to arguments about the truth of Christianity?

I realized that the answers to these questions were found in the work of grace, starting much further back in my life than I had at first realized. More needed to be said about the early stages of my journey.

As I became increasingly involved in apologetics, I also recognized the importance of imagination as both the catalyst and the foundation of my rational exploration of the Faith. It was imagination that made Christian concepts meaningful to me. Until words like 'God' and 'Jesus' and 'Resurrection' became meaningful—literally, filled with meaning—rather than abstract signifiers, arguments about religion were just intellectual games, with no real-world significance.

Too often in apologetics today, Christians are tempted to look for the silver-bullet argument, the right thing to say at the right time so that the other person will concede, "I've been completely wrong all along! Give me a Bible!" Or worse, apologists may treat argument as a rhetorical kung fu move to 'defeat' or 'crush' an atheist. Other times, Christians press people to recognize the existence of God and acknowledge their own sinfulness, quickly declaring it evidence of hardness of heart when the sceptic resists. We forget that the Christian and the unbeliever often lack shared meaning for words like 'God' and 'sin'. All too often, we talk past the very people we are trying to help.

We need an appreciation of the way reason and imagination interact, and the way that meaning is wrestled with and formed over the long term. Without such an understanding, apologists can easily become frustrated when providing a compelling argument, decisively refuting an objection, or providing Scriptural backup doesn't lead to an immediate conversion. A well-intentioned desire to share the truth can turn into arrogant impatience: "Can't you see how obviously wrong you are? Your objections are invalid. Get with the program and be converted already!"

If we are effectively to communicate the gospel to more than a tiny percentage of people today, and help Christians have a robust and lasting and transformative relationship with Christ, we need to be in it for the long haul, with the ability to use both rational and imaginative approaches to questions of belief and practice.

And so, I started thinking about how I'd talked about my journey to faith, what I'd included, what I'd left out, what I'd merely hinted at. I came to see that those few months of intense research and reflection in which I reconsidered my atheism did not mark so much a change, as a tipping point. When I encountered arguments and evidence for Christianity, my reason was finally able to align with my imagination, which, like a compass needle, had tremulously pointed toward true north for many years.

With the opportunity to give a fuller account of my conversion to Christianity came the opportunity also to tell how my story has continued to unfold. By the grace of God, my story has been that of gradually loving God more fully and more deeply, and of continuing to follow his truth wherever it led, which, as it turned out, was into the Catholic Church.

"Expect the unexpected" seems to be a useful approach to the Christian life. When I wrote the first version of the book, I was an Episcopalian and a tenured English professor in Southern California, getting an apologetics degree from a Protestant university; as I write this, I am a Catholic and director of the M.A. in Cultural Apologetics at Houston Baptist University in Texas. You can't make this stuff up ...

So, then, this book looks both forward and backward from that first snapshot of my journey given in *Not God's Type*. Forward, to 'crossing the Tiber' and being received into full communion with the Catholic Church; and backward, to trace the deeper roots of both my atheism and my faith.

Chapter I

A GLORIOUS DEFEAT

It seemed I saw a tree, more marvelous than any other,
Lifted on high, all wound about with light,
Brightest of crosses. That beacon
Gleamed with gold. Gems
Were scattered shining at its foot; and
Five were fixed upon the crossbeams.

— "The Dream of the Rood"

Here I set out to do what might seem to be a straightforward task: to recount how it happened that I walked away from atheism and entered into Christian faith.

But the story is not a simple one to tell.

When I said Yes to Christ, I thought I had reached the end of my journey, but I found that I had merely crested the nearest hill. The road, it seemed, went ever on and on, and I soon realized that the Christian life was not going to be easy.

It was exciting to learn more about theology and doctrine—go figure, I'm an academic—but assimilating this new knowledge into my daily life was much harder. I had to learn how to pray, and how to be part of a community with these strange and slightly scary people called 'Christians'. I had to reevaluate my position as a liberal feminist; much of what I had believed turned out to be false, grounded as it was in an incomplete and distorted understanding of what it means to be human (and female). I had to discover how to be a Christian witness in a hostile environment, as an English professor at a secular community college.

And I had to learn to see myself in a new way. I had considered myself to be reasonably 'nice' and 'good', but now I understood that even at my very best I fell infinitely short of the perfection of God, the source of all goodness. Yet the Church taught that my heavenly Father loves me completely and unreservedly. In the light of that unmerited love, I formed the desire for a stronger and deeper relationship with my Savior and for his help to become the woman he made me to be.

Perhaps the most difficult, and most transformative, part of my new life was that I was brought for the first time, and then repeatedly, to the foot of the Cross; it was there that I discovered the reality of grace.

At the time I became a Christian, outwardly I seemed to have my act together. But I was inwardly wounded, having just come out of a disastrous long-term relationship, one that had been wrongly entered into—as the Church teaches, though I didn't know it at the time—and painfully ended.

Could God's grace reach and heal the hidden wounds of my heart? I didn't know enough even to ask the question; I was still too numbed to know how badly I needed help. In my journey to Christian faith, I had focused on the Resurrection; but after my baptism, that sacramental entry into the death and Resurrection of Christ, I began to discover that the Cross is the fount of healing and transforming grace: not just part of the historical events of Jesus' Passion and death, but the place where the Incarnate God took all the black weight of human misery, and broke its power for everyone; for me.

The Cross, to put it bluntly, is where all the sh—— stops. All of it. There are so many ways that one human being can hurt another, so many petty cruelties, abuses of power, belittling words; I felt the drop-by-drop accumulation of mundane misery until I feared that I would drown and began almost to wish that I would. Loneliness, betrayal, anxiety, and depression cut deep and don't always leave outward marks. But all suffering is taken up on the Cross and finds its place in the mark of the nails in Christ's hands and feet, the gash in his side: five precious wounds that he bears now and forever in his risen and glorified body.

"This is my body, which will be given up for you." Not a grace too fine and spiritual for me to grasp, but flesh and blood, bread and wine, given for me; touching, transforming, renewing mind, body, soul. Not all at once, but slowly, like the coming of spring in my New England childhood: one day, the ground is squelchy-soft with melting snow; one day, a haze of green is on the tips of winter-stark branches; one day, a bright-eyed robin hops across the lawn, and winter has passed; the summer will come true.

This narrative does not pretend to have photographic precision. I cannot depict exactly how things were because words can only do so much and, in any case, I am not the person I was then. Although I'm close enough to remember much of how I felt and thought, the changes I've gone through really have been changes.

More importantly, the meaning of my journey to faith has unfolded further as time has gone on. I have come to see aspects of my experiences that I did not notice and indeed could not have noticed at the time. I have begun to recognize the way that grace had been infusing my imagination for many years without my realizing it, like a river that ran deep below the surface of a desert, until one day, to the great surprise of the weary traveler, it bubbled to the surface, clear and sweet and cool.

So then: this is the account of a glorious defeat, an unsought but desperately needed relinquishing of my cherished independence—an unconditional surrender in which I was brought from death to life, from trying to live without God to being led fully into his Body, the Church. And as I first knew Christ as my sovereign Lord, this is also a sketch of how I later grew to love him as my Savior.

Lastly, this is not, at the heart of it, a story of what I was clever enough to do, but rather of what I was weak enough to have done to me and for me. It is an account of God's work, a tale of grace acting in and through human beings but always issuing from him and leading back to him. And it is the story of my being brought home.

Chapter 2

THE DARK WOOD

In the midway of this our mortal life,
I found me in a gloomy wood, astray
Gone from the path direct: and e'en to tell
It were no easy task, how savage wild
That forest, how robust and rough its growth,
Which to remember only, my dismay
Renews, in bitterness not far from death.

—Dante, *The Divine Comedy: Hell*

The word 'atheist' comes from the Greek *a theos*; literally, 'without God'.

That is how I would have described myself at thirty-one years old, nearly the same age as Dante in the Dark Wood. I was an atheist college professor, and I delighted in thinking of myself that way. I got a kick out of being an unbeliever; it was fun to consider myself superior to the unenlightened, superstitious masses and to make snide comments about Christians.

I thought I was completely without faith. Certainly, I would have told anyone who asked that I was not looking for God, and this was a true statement as I understood it then. I was looking for *something*—purpose, meaning, satisfaction— but since I did not then believe that God existed, it did not (and indeed could not) occur to me that what I was searching for would be found in God.

When I was eight or nine years old, it came to my parents' attention that my distance vision was very poor: my teachers had observed me squinting at the blackboard and moving all the way up to the front row to copy homework assignments into my notebook. I'd never thought twice about it. Of course things were fuzzy when they're more than a few inches away; wasn't it like that for everyone? No, apparently not. That evening, to help me understand, my brother handed me his glasses and told me to look through them.

It was near Christmas, and what I first looked at was the Christmas tree, festooned with its strings of colored lights. I was amazed: the familiar blurry color-bursts resolved into sharp-edged sparkles. Looking up, for the first time I could see the details of the ornaments hanging above my head, the red stripe around the edges of the tree-top star.

Now, as an adult, I'm slightly on edge if I *don't* wear my eyeglasses all the time—perhaps because of one-too-many encounters with an innocuous-seeming black fuzz that on close-up turned out to be a spider! As a child, though, I was a little bit frightened by that first transformation of vision. The world had lost its soft edges. There was more to take in than I'd expected. Eventually I got used to my new glasses, and appreciated how much more I could see and do. But until I looked through my brother's pair, I'd never even guessed that the world could look different than it did.

Such was my life as an atheist. Now when I consider my life before I knew Christ, I recognize how limited my vision was. I desperately needed God's presence in my life, but I would have flatly, uncomprehendingly, denied any such need.

My problem could not be solved by hearing a preacher assert that Jesus loved me and wanted to save me. I didn't believe in God to begin with, and I assumed that the Bible was a collection of folktales and myths, like the stories I'd read of Zeus and Thor, Cinderella and Sleeping Beauty, only not so interesting. Why should I bother to read the Bible, much less take seriously what it said about this Jesus? I certainly didn't think an imaginary God could have a real Son. Since I didn't believe that I had an immortal soul, I wasn't in the least interested in its purported destination after I died. No God, no afterlife, no hell ... no reason to discuss the matter further.

The difficulty was not a lack of opportunity to hear about God. The problem lay deeper: in my very concept of what faith was. I thought faith was by definition irrational, that it meant believing some assertion to be true for no reason. It had never occurred to me that there could be a path to faith in God involving reason, or that there might be evidence for the claims of Christianity. I thought you had to 'just have faith'—and the very idea of faith baffled and horrified me.

Even so, it was an idea that stuck with me. I didn't have faith, I didn't want faith, but I felt compelled to have a good reason why not. I constructed an elaborate analogy for myself, one that I felt gave a satisfying explanation of why faith was impossible.

I set it up like this: imagine that you tell me, "If you believe that there's an invisible pink unicorn in the sky, I'll give you a new BMW." I see the car in the parking lot; you jingle the keys in your hands. If I can believe what you want me to believe, the new car is mine. Cool! But it's a waste of time: I know there's no unicorn. No matter how much I want that car, I am incapable of believing something contrary to reason in order to get it.

Believing something irrational on demand to get a prize: that is what the evangelical invitation to "accept Jesus and get eternal life in heaven!" sounded like to me.

This impossible invitation was made all the more baffling by the fact that the prize didn't sound very inviting to begin with. What was this 'heaven' anyway? While the mere name of the 'Elysian Fields' from Greek mythology conjured up an expansive sunlit landscape in my mind's eye, and the Norse 'Valhalla' evoked a colorful picture of warriors feasting and singing songs, the Christian 'heaven' was associated (thanks largely to television) with the image of blandly smiling people in white robes standing around with nothing much to do. I was supposed to get excited about this?

Still: even if I took Christians at their word that 'heaven' was desirable, I simply *couldn't* believe.

Sure, if I thought I could benefit by it, I could pretend to believe, and say so: "Oh, yes, I believe in Jesus!" But I'd know I was lying, which would make this so-called 'faith' a deliberate, repellent falsehood.

The only other option, I thought, would be to try to convince myself that I believed. Indeed I might be able to work myself up into such a pitch of desire for the product on offer that I could, for a time, *believe that I believed*. But it wouldn't be the same thing as really believing—and the idea that I ought to make the effort seemed disgusting and immoral. As I understood it, then, faith was at best a delusion and at worst total hypocrisy.

To me, the decisive argument against faith was that I *could not* believe, no matter how much I might want to. If God did exist and would punish me for not believing, I was stuck with being punished. I thought 'faith' was a meaningless word, that so-called believers were either hypocrites or self-deluded fools, and that it was a waste of time even to consider any claim a Christian made about the truth.

Given what I thought faith to be, and given the reprehensible state of my knowledge about Christianity, I concluded (not entirely unreasonably) that I had better things to do with my time than investigate somebody's shopworn just-so stories. There were plenty of things that people cared deeply about, perhaps even believed to be true, that I felt no inclination to explore: Buddhism, veganism, string theory, Marxism, reincarnation, the literary merit of James Joyce ... Christianity was just one more of these topics that I saw no reason to bother with.

If I had inquired, I would have found the Bible was nothing like I thought it was. I would have encountered Saint Paul's forthright declaration that Christianity is based on the historical, witnessed events of Christ's death and Resurrection. I would have discovered that theology and philosophy offered thoughtful, complex answers to my questions, not a simplistic appeal to blind faith. I would have realized that the art, literature, and music that moved me most deeply was grounded in a Christian understanding of the world. I would have found that the Church's two-thousand-year history did not conform to my image of the Christian faith as a self-serving, politically useful fiction.

But I thought I knew exactly what faith was, and so I declined to look further. Or perhaps I was afraid that there was more to faith than I was willing to credit, and I didn't want to deal with it. Easier by far to read only books by atheists that told me what I wanted to hear: that I was smarter and more intellectually honest than the poor, deluded Christians.

I had built myself a fortress of atheism, secure against any attack by irrational faith. And I lived in it, alone.

Chapter 3

ALONE IN THE FORTRESS
OF ATHEISM

[After the theft of the Sun and Moon] the frost came and killed the crops, and the cattle began to die of hunger. Every living thing felt sick and faint in the dark, dreary world. Then one of the maidens of Kalevala suggested to Ilmarinen to make a moon of gold and a sun of silver, and to hang them up in the heavens; so Ilmarinen set to work. While he was forging them, Wainamoinen came and asked what he was working at, and so Ilmarinen told him that he was going to make a new sun and moon. But Wainamoinen said: "This is mere folly, for silver and gold will not shine like the sun and moon." Still Ilmarinen worked on, and at length he had forged a moon of gold and a sun of silver, and hung them in their places in the sky. But they gave no light, as Wainamoinen had said.

— *Finnish Legends for English Children*

Life inside the fortress of atheism was good. I thought I could make sense of the world just as well as, or much better than, the people who claimed to have faith. I didn't believe in God, but I had a worldview that felt perfectly satisfactory. It wasn't a particularly cheery view, but I preferred truth over comfort any day.

What, then, did I believe?

I held that I was the product of blind chance working over millions of years, a member of a species that happened to be more intelligent than other mammals but was not unique. I thought I was a social creature because that was how humans evolved; the language that I delighted in using was just a tool that humans had developed along the way.

If I had been consistent, I would have embraced the theories of literary criticism that treated stories and poems as language games with no meaning outside the text, or that pronounced language itself to be self-contradictory and meaningless, but I didn't; one of the reasons I wrote my doctoral dissertation on the little-regarded genre of fantasy was that I wanted to avoid that kind of literary theory and stick to a more traditional, meaning-based interpretation of the books. Even though in doing so I was contradicting the principles that undergirded my atheism, I treated art, music, and literature as if they had real meaning. I studiously avoided thinking through why I did this.

I did not believe that human beings had souls. I thought that when I died, my consciousness would simply switch off, and that the only immortality in store for me was that of my body decaying and returning its constituent atoms for other living beings to use; sometimes I even thought that was a beautiful and consoling prospect. I vaguely thought of 'personhood' as defined by self-awareness and intelligence, though I found that this position raised disturbing questions. I thought abortion was acceptable, but how was that so different from infanticide? If what made a genuine 'person' was a functioning mind and body, were the lives of the profoundly disabled or the mentally handicapped meaningful at all? Once the mind was gone, did a person have a right to live? One day I caught myself thinking favorably about euthanasia for the severely handicapped. Although I backed away from the idea immediately, I felt queasy that I'd taken it seriously even for a moment. I was aware that there was something badly wrong with the reasoning that led to ideas like this, but I preferred not to think about why.

Behind all of my consciously articulated views was the same premise: there is no God, no ultimate meaning beyond ourselves.

If there is no real meaning to our lives, what is the point of living? As early as high school, I had recognized the problem. I remember in my junior-year Latin class reading some of the more philosophically despairing poets, and asking my teacher why, if they felt life was meaningless, didn't they just kill themselves? My teacher replied, "A lot of them did."

Even so, I believed that it was possible and desirable to be a good person (never mind the question of where my standard of 'goodness' came from). I thought that life was worth living, even when it was difficult. How could it be so and yet have no meaning?

Atheism, when consistently lived out, leads to self-deception or despair. Self-constructed meaning is only a stop-gap: it is real only in the sense that a stage set of Elsinore Castle is a real place. One can suspend disbelief while *Hamlet* is being performed, but at some point, the curtain falls and one must leave the theater. What's to be done when Helping Others, Doing Good Work, and Having Friends are recognized as paint and canvas and trick lighting?

It was tempting to make atheism into a larger cause for the benefit of mankind. Perhaps it would be worth devoting one's life to creating a world without religion, blissfully free from the chains of superstition. It's the vision that John Lennon captures in "Imagine", and it's beautiful ... if you try not to think too hard about it. As Francis Spufford puts it:

consider the teased and coiffed nylon monument that is 'Imagine': surely the My Little Pony of philosophical statements. . . . Imagine there's no heaven. Imagine there's no hell. Imagine all the people, living life in—hello? Excuse me? Take religion out of the picture, and everybody spontaneously starts living life in *peace*? I don't know about you, but in my experience peace is not the default state of human beings.

All I had to do was look at myself and the people around me to recognize that anger, jealousy, insecurity, envy, contempt, selfishness, fear, and greed were deeply rooted in the soil of being human. It seemed to me that a universal embrace of atheism would leave people with all the same problems as before, if not worse (I was not unaware that the human-rights track record of dogmatically atheist countries was, shall we say, poor). I knew the difference between imagination and wishful thinking. Atheism might be true, but pretending it was a humanitarian cause offered no solution to my problems.

What to do?

When the alternative is succumbing to darkness, anything seems worth a try. In his poem "Dover Beach" Matthew Arnold confronts a world in which beauty and meaning have proved to be mere wishes and false hopes:

> [T]he world, which seems
> To lie before us like a land of dreams,
> So various, so beautiful, so new,
> Hath really neither joy, nor love, nor light,
> Nor certitude, nor help for pain;
> And we are here as on a darkling plain
> Swept with confused alarms of struggle and flight,
> Where ignorant armies clash by night.

Faced with this bleak vision, he cries out, "Ah, love, let us be true / To one another!" To a young would-be romantic, that sounds like a pretty good solution. The only problem is that any couple relying exclusively on each other for all their fulfillment and meaning will surely drown, as Shakespeare says, like "two spent swimmers that do cling together / And choke their art."

As for me, I tried to hold the darkness at bay by seeking meaning in activities that I deemed worthwhile: teaching, appreciating literature, winning fencing tournaments, writing a book, saving and investing money. These were things that were good in themselves, at least to an extent, and there was no obvious downside to looking for my life's meaning in them.

And yet, no matter what I turned my hand to, I found satisfaction in nothing. I wanted to be a good teacher, but I felt my students did not cooperate. I wanted them to be grateful and appreciative, but instead they were so very needy, demanding patience and self-control and concern far beyond my capacity to give. I became frustrated; I shirked my responsibilities to my colleagues; I resented my misbehaving students. One day I found myself screaming, livid with anger, at a class of freshmen who would not, simply *would not*, stop talking in class. With terrible clarity, I saw and despised the person I was becoming—and I felt powerless to stop the change.

Fencing was a saving grace.

I had been fencing sabre competitively since college, and I loved it. Of the three fencing weapons (foil, épée, and sabre), sabre is the most dynamic and fast-paced. When I started fencing, it was also almost exclusively a man's sport. In fact, I had been on the *men's* sabre squad in college—there was no women's squad. I was proud of being a woman on the forefront of the sport; it gave me a sense of accomplishment.

As a petite woman sabrist, I had to be brave: my opponents were almost always bigger and stronger than I was. I had to be focused: the tactical possibilities unfold at dizzying speed during a bout. And I had to be tough: despite protective gear, getting hit full speed, full strength with a three-foot-long flexible steel blade *hurts*.

Even when I was troubled and conflicted in the rest of my life, I could feel fully myself while fencing. The sport had a beauty all its own, found in the satisfying steel-on-steel of a perfect parry-riposte, in the athletic dance of advance, retreat, lunge. On the fencing strip, there was nowhere to hide: you landed the touch, or did not; you won the bout, or lost. There was a clarity in the physical and mental demands of fencing that allowed me, there and nowhere else, to acknowledge being something less than I wanted to be, and to feel like the effort to improve myself mattered—at least for a little while.

But fencing only ameliorated my struggle with darkness; it did not resolve it.

Increasingly, the view was clear: if life truly has no meaning, then our actions cannot themselves have any meaning either.

And so I came gradually to another way to manage despair: pride. I began to lean on my sense of my own intellectual strength. All right, I said to myself, when we die, we die; nothing that we do has any ultimate meaning. So be it! I could take a certain grim satisfaction in facing the facts. Weak and sentimental people might scurry to the cover of some 'faith' that allowed them to pretend otherwise; I would be strong and resolute. I would look into the abyss, and let the abyss look back, and carry on.

In its own way, this was a satisfying position. I could feel superior to anyone—certainly to Christians, whom I viewed as weak and unable to face the truth. I began to conceive of life as a great tragedy, our little conscious lives like tiny candle flames in the night, with despair looming in the flickering shadows. The bedrock of my ideology became the defiant cry: there is no meaning! Some fools couldn't face the darkness, but as for me, I could savor the idea of standing on my lonely precipice, able to recognize my identity as a meaningless speck in an uncaring universe and go on living without the artificial comforts of religion.

This is a despairing pride, a lonely pride, and ultimately an alienating pride, but it provided a dark kind of solace. Feeling superior is terribly seductive. Once you are there, it is hard to back down. To retreat from the precipice of despair would mean that 'those people' whom you have so enjoyed sneering at really did know more than you. It would mean giving up the intoxicating sense of being special by virtue of everyone else being a fool.

Yet I was troubled by what I knew of myself. I sensed that the pride that sustained me was somehow unhealthy; it connected too easily to contempt and predisposed me to isolation. I knew I was prone to intense anger, perhaps all the more terrible because I almost never let it show. I once lost my temper at a fencing tournament and in a split-second response vented my anger by hitting my opponent so hard on the mask that my sabre broke. I was frightened by my own loss of control, so I pretended that it had happened accidentally, but I knew it had been deliberate. Whenever I glanced into the deep pit of anger in my heart, I knew that all was not well.

My atheism was eating into my heart like acid. On 9/11 I was genuinely shocked by that vicious destruction of innocent life, until I began to rationalize myself out of my emotional reaction. What did these people matter to me? Weren't thousands killed every year in automobile accidents? Why should I grieve for strangers? It worked; I stopped caring. At the same time, I was dully horrified at my dismissal of something that I knew objectively deserved a response of grief and sorrow. In a transitory moment of insight, I recognized my condition as numbness, not superior rationality.

However satisfied I declared myself intellectually, however impregnable this intellectual fortress of atheism seemed to me, it was a grim place to live. Even as I grew more intellectually enamored of atheism, I found myself having a harder time living in the light of its conclusions.

What I didn't realize at the time was how inconsistent I was. I could not have explained the source of my own rationality, nor of my conviction that there were such things as truth, beauty, and goodness. I used the language of morality, even as I argued that the Source of all morality did not exist. Though I felt comfortable being the final arbiter of what was 'good enough' in terms of my own behavior, I was sure that the words 'good' and 'evil' referred to real things, and that I ought to strive for the good, even if it didn't benefit me personally.

Although my creed held that there was no ultimate meaning, I stubbornly believed that there was such a thing as truth, and I valued truth as an absolute good. That is precisely why I so firmly rejected what I thought faith was: making yourself believe something comforting but untrue. I believed that if there were no meaning and no hope, then the right and good thing to do would be to confront that truth and not try to hide from it. I wanted to know, and live by, the truth—no matter what.

Yet my very idea of truth precluded any consideration of Christianity. As I understood faith, *by definition* it was irrational, and thus by definition it could not help me in the only way that I would accept help.

Thus, when I was so firmly an atheist, I would not—and could not—have listened to and understood the arguments that ultimately convinced me. I had locked myself into my fortress and flung away the key.

But even a fortress may have windows; and over it is the sky; and its stones rest on the good earth ...

Interlude 1

It was my third year as a Christian and, as the Church moved through the liturgical cycle of the life of Christ, I looked forward once again to its culmination in Holy Week: the solemnity and drama of the movement through Palm Sunday, Maundy Thursday, Good Friday, and then, at last, joyous Easter, the Resurrection of our Lord.

St. Michael's by-the-Sea had a lively ministry of members of the congregation who read the Scripture lessons at church services. A few months before, I'd begun serving as a reader once a week at Evening Prayer. Then, shortly before Easter, one of the readers for the Holy Week services was unexpectedly called out of town, and I was asked to fill in. Who, me? Yes, you.

And so it was that on Good Friday I found myself standing at the lectern before a packed church. I led the reading of the penitential Psalm 51, and then began to read the liturgy of the Prayers of the People.

"Let us pray for all nations and peoples of the earth, and for those in authority among them, that by God's help they may seek justice and truth, and live in peace and concord . . ."

The church on Good Friday was a solemn place. The walls were bare, the banners having been taken down at the start of Lent. The altar had been stripped of all its linens. The great crucifix over the altar was veiled. During this service, no bells were rung, no hymns were sung; we entered and left in silence.

"Let us pray for all who suffer and are afflicted in body
or in mind, that God in His mercy will comfort and relieve
them, and grant them the knowledge of His love, and stir up
in us the will and patience to minister to their needs ..."

As I read the prayers on behalf of the congregation, I felt
deeply that indeed it was not 'me' and 'them' in prayer, but
'us'.

"Let us pray for all who have not received the Gospel of
Christ ..."

I had heard these words before, in the Good Friday service each of the two previous years. Once again, it struck me
powerfully that this was not just a general prayer for the lost:
it had been a prayer for me.

"... for those who have never heard the word of salvation ..."

Did the people of St. Michael's have any idea that, in the
years before, as they had prayed this same liturgy, they had
been praying for me?

"... for those hardened by sin or indifference; for the con-
temptuous and the scornful; for those who are enemies of the
cross of Christ and persecutors of his disciples ..."

I heard my voice shaking as I finished:

"... that God will open their hearts to the truth, and lead
them to faith and obedience."

How easy it would have been to write me off: a lost cause,
a waste of time, an enemy of Christ. And yet, I had been
prayed for, by those who knew me and by those who did
not. For just a moment, I sensed a living web of prayer, bright
and strong, connecting past, present, and future, far and near.

Chapter 4

THE INVISIBLE LAMP

You create a world, [a reader wrote to Tolkien] in which some sort of faith seems to be everywhere without a visible source, like light from an invisible lamp.

— *The Letters of J. R. R. Tolkien*

As an atheist, I would have said that faith of any kind was alien to me, and had been alien to me since as far back as I could recall. I had never in my life said a prayer, never been to a church service.

A memory from first grade seemed iconic: the teacher giving us children words to spell on the chalkboard. I was a precocious reader and writer, so I wrote my word confidently: "g-o-d". But the little boy next to me who wrote "G-o-d" was praised for his correct spelling, not me. From my storybooks on Greek and Norse myths I was familiar with lots of gods, and so the capital G puzzled me. I did not understand that God could be a name.

In one sense, I had a nonreligious childhood. Easter meant chocolate bunnies; Christmas meant presents. Yet, although I remember only a few of the Christmas gifts I received over the years, I vividly recall the festivity of the season. Sugar cookies and gingerbread men, never made at any other time of the year. Putting the tree up the day after Thanksgiving:

none of this waiting-till-the-last-minute nonsense. (Yes, it was an artificial tree—not as authentic, but less messy. If some families had a tradition of going to pick out the tree and bring it home, our family's tradition was Help Dad Assemble the Tree.)

At night, I'd sometimes scoot on my back under the tree, gazing up through the branches all decked with tiny colored lights; or I'd sit in the dark and look at the colors dappling onto the walls and ceiling, feathered with shadows from the needled branches. It made my heart ache with its beauty, and with a sense of wonder and awe that I could not have put into words.

My mom rarely put music on the stereo during the rest of the year, but during the month leading up to Christmas—the time that the Church marks as Advent, though I didn't know anything of liturgical seasons then—she would play Christmas records, and the house was full of songs and carols. "Silent Night", "We Three Kings", "God Rest Ye Merry, Gentlemen", "O Come All Ye Faithful", "Silver Bells", and my favorite, "Hark! The Herald Angels Sing".

When I finally became a Christian, I had to learn everything from the Lord's Prayer onward. But when I celebrated my first Christmas as a Christian, I was delighted to find that I already knew many of the hymns for this season!

I never gave thought to whether these carols were about something that really happened. It wasn't that I believed they were false; the question never occurred to me one way or the other. I knew nothing about Jesus, and didn't go to church. I had neither the content of faith nor the practice of it, but the music formed a little space in my soul, like a cup waiting to be filled, that by its very shape suggested something was meant to go there.

I was fascinated, too, by my family's Nativity set. Out it came every year, totally without explanation, a wooden

Nativity made in Bethlehem. There was Mary, Joseph, the baby Jesus, the three Wise Men and their camels, and—what I liked best—cows and a dozen or so tiny sheep and their shepherd; I didn't play with them, but I liked to move them about in different arrangements around the central manger. The figures were unpainted and roughly carved, but they were somehow imaginatively suggestive. Here was a story.

It was a seed that lay dormant for a long time, but it was a seed.

As I grew up, I had a parallel life of the imagination, running alongside the outward and visible life of experiences with school and friends and family: I loved to read.

I am very introverted, with an abundant share of native New England reserve, and as a child I was shy and anxious about new people and new situations (I still am). But in books I explored a vast, dynamic, endlessly interesting world, and I responded to that world creatively by writing, drawing pictures, creating elaborate sets of paper animals and paper people to play out my own imagined stories, from migrating caribou, to knights and dragons and battles, to families shipwrecked on desert isles.

A love of reading was the very best gift of my childhood. In retrospect I realize that we were quite poor when I was growing up; my dad was in the Air Force and the military have never been paid lavishly. Neither of my parents had a college education, but they were both avid readers, there were books everywhere in the house, and I was read to regularly until I learned how to read on my own. We had family trips to the library every week, on bicycles or in the car, returning with stacks of books.

What did I read? My favorites still resonate in my memory. *The Wind in the Willows*. The Little House on the Prairie series. *Black Beauty*. *Little Women*. The Greek myths, in a collection called *Myths Every Child Should Know*. *Alice in*

Wonderland, with Tenniel's illustrations. *Swiss Family Robinson*. The stories of Hans Christian Andersen. The Chronicles of Narnia. *In the Days of the Giants*, a collection of Norse myths in an antique volume with illustrations.

Then, delight of delights, when I was about ten years old, my parents got me a subscription to the Time-Life series The Enchanted World: every month or two, a new volume arrived in the mail. Cloth-bound in jewel-bright colors, with vivid and evocative pictures, these volumes opened up the world of myth and fantasy and folklore: *Fairies and Elves, King Arthur, Ghosts, Wizards, Magical Beasts* ... I pored over those books for hours, and they opened up into a wider world of literary imaginings that I would later explore with delight as an adult: *The Mabinogion, The Kalevala, The Morte d'Arthur.*

Long before I gave any thought about whether Christianity was true, and long before I considered questions of faith and practice, my imagination was being fed Christianly. I delighted in the stories of King Arthur's knights and the quest for the Holy Grail, without knowing that the Grail was the cup from the Last Supper. I had no idea that the Chronicles of Narnia had anything to do with Jesus, but images from the stories stuck with me, as bright and vivid in my memory as if I had caught sight of a real landscape, had a real encounter, with more significance than I could quite grasp.

And at some point in my childhood, I found J. R. R. Tolkien's *The Hobbit* and *The Lord of the Rings*, and that changed everything. Not suddenly. Not even immediately. But slowly, surely. Like light from an invisible lamp, God's grace was beginning to shine out from Tolkien's works, illuminating my godless imagination with a Christian vision.

I don't remember reading *The Lord of the Rings* and *The Hobbit* for the first time, only rereading them again and again.

Imaginatively, Tolkien's Middle-earth always felt right; it had the ordinary pleasures and disappointments of life as well as the high excitements and fears. It had a place for both hope and disappointment, achievement and failure. Like the world I lived in, Middle-earth had greater depths than I could take in at any given moment. It was a world in which there is darkness, but also real light, a light that shines in the darkness and is not extinguished: Galadriel's light, and the light of the star that Sam sees break through the clouds in Mordor, and the ray of sun that falls on the flower-crowned head of the king's broken statue at the crossroads.

The Lord of the Rings was where I first encountered the *evangelium*, the good news. I didn't know, then, that my imagination had been, as it were, baptized in Middle-earth. But something took root in my reading of Tolkien that would flower many years later.

In the meantime, the story-world that captured my imagination from about age ten to thirteen was Anne McCaffrey's Dragonriders of Pern series, with its fire-breathing dragons and valiant dragonriders. I loved the idea of having a huge, beautiful dragon as a friend-for-life, to whom you (and only you) could speak telepathically. McCaffrey's world appealed to two of the great longings that Tolkien names, the desire to fly like birds and to communicate with animals.

But Pern was also a world of insiders and outsiders. Only a select few were chosen to be dragonrider candidates, and fewer still were chosen by newly hatched dragons. Those who had adventures were already special, their superiority simply waiting to be recognized. When I imagined myself into Pern, it had to be as a movie-star version of myself: athletic, assertive, witty, attractively dangerous, and either (a) popular or (b) so self-confident as to not care about popularity. There was no space for me as myself, an ordinary girl.

Lucy Pevensie wouldn't have fit in, either. Maybe that's why I could breathe easily in Narnia the way I couldn't in Pern.

As a teenager, I looked for an imaginative world that would help me make sense of the anxiety and uncertainty that I felt, about to go to college and live away from home for the first time, faced with the need to live up to the potential that everyone seemed to see in me, the straight-A, Honor Society student.

I became fascinated for a time by Harlan Ellison, whose bleak, angry science-fiction stories voiced something I had finally noticed: that there was something profoundly wrong with the world, and specifically something wrong with *people*. Beyond my own experiences of being teased and left out (being the 'shy girl with thick glasses who skipped a grade' is not exactly a ticket to popularity), I discovered a whole panorama of human wickedness, from the horrors of the Holocaust to the slaughter of the great whales, from neglected and abused pets to people being mugged and murdered on the streets of New York. I cared deeply, such that I wished I did not care, because I saw no way that anything I could do would be a bit of good. Ellison's rage-filled shouts against the cruelty of the world were bitterly satisfying for a while, but they palled. Beneath the anger there was nothing solid.

Star Trek moved into center stage as my imaginative world of choice, offering a bright, clean, adventurous future. Captain Picard became my hero, a man of intellect, integrity, and decisive action. The crew had adventures, teased one another, and stuck together through thick and thin. Even when they encountered a morally troubling situation, it still fit into the framework of an orderly, fundamentally safe universe.

There's a bottomless well of *Star Trek* fandom out there, and I drank deeply from it. I read scores of cheesy *Trek* novels, wrote fan-fiction, and attended *Star Trek* conventions, where half the attendees were in costume. I was looking for something, and this was close, but ... it still didn't satisfy. I kept going to the conventions, but they became less and less interesting. In retrospect, the problem was this: you can't buy a phaser or a tricorder; you can only buy a toy that makes a noise like the one on the show. You can't buy a tribble as a pet; you can only get a fake-fur ball with a battery-operated purr motor. The very existence of these material props is a reminder that *Star Trek* is *not* a real world.

I wanted the real thing: real adventure, real meaning, real belonging. I didn't know where to find it—or if it even existed.

Chapter 5

THE PEN AND THE SWORD

"I caught him, with an unseen hook and an invisible line which is long enough to let him wander to the ends of the world, and still to bring him back with a twitch upon the thread."

—G. K. Chesterton, *The Innocence of Father Brown*

At seventeen I went off to college. I had developed the same incuriosity about religion that I had for other activities that didn't interest me, like golf or chess. Even so, just as I could have been convinced that golf had some merits as a game (miniature golf was fun, after all), I wasn't entirely antagonistic to religion, per se.

My first winter at college, I took it into my head to celebrate Yule, trudging out into a snowy patch of woods by the dorms one evening to light a candle in an act of unspecified spirituality. I got cold, and no revelation was vouchsafed to me from Mother Nature, but the woods were beautiful, so I didn't mind.

The door was still open; but it was soon to close.

In college, I absorbed the idea that Christianity was a historical artifact or a blemish on modern civilization or perhaps both. My science classes implied that Christians were anti-intellectuals who were to be pitied for their superstitious rejection of Darwinism. My anthropology classes presented Christian missionaries as narrow-minded colonialists who extinguished authentic expressions of native religion. (I did not quite know what to think about the integral part that human sacrifice played in the authentic expression of the Aztec religion.) My history and literature classes omitted or downplayed references to historical figures' faith, as if their beliefs were entirely private and subjective.

I remember an upper-division English literature class on Chaucer's *Canterbury Tales*. We discussed his criticism of corruption and hypocrisy in the medieval church, without considering the faith that would move people to go on a pilgrimage in the first place; I was left with the impression that Chaucer was a forward-thinking humanist, not a believing Christian. I never noticed that Chaucer asks readers to give thanks for anything valuable in the poem to "Our Lord Jesus Christ ... from whom proceeds all understanding and goodness."

I suppose I must have had classmates or professors who were Christians, but if I did, I never knew any of them. Nobody talked about faith or Christianity on campus. I remember one particular girl in my dorm, first semester freshman year, who (as I realize in retrospect) was probably a Christian; she objected to the fact that the resident assistants distributed free condoms and had mandatory dorm meetings in which we were instructed on how to do things safely that I, at least, had never even imagined that people did at all. The objecting girl was nice, though I didn't understand why she was making such a big deal about all this; then she moved off-campus, and I forgot about her.

I'd seen people handing out pamphlets and telling passers-by "Jesus loves you!" or holding up signs at football games that said "John 3:16", which baffled me entirely (I thought it must be some sort of code). I only knew the word 'evange-list' in the form of 'televangelist', which I associated with bad fashion and pathetic scandals. I did not know anything about Christianity, and why bother learning?

Yet in college, I also encountered the poet who would, more than any other writer except Tolkien, influence the course of my life: the Catholic poet and priest Gerard Manley Hopkins.

I first read Hopkins as a sophomore, in the mandatory-for-English-majors class British Writers II, his poems in the brick-shaped and brick-heavy *Norton Anthology of English Literature*, with its tissue-thin paper and narrow margins. I'd been a bit skittish about the course because my exposure to poetry had hitherto been exclusively in the classroom, where we had studied What Poems Meant and What Things Symbolized—a far cry from the effortless immersion in Story that I knew and loved as a private reader of novels.

Enter Professor Keefe. I suppose we talked about the meaning of the poetry we read in his class—Keats, Browning, Shelley, Hopkins, Blake—but what I remember was the way he read poetry to us out loud. I was mesmerized. I hadn't been read to aloud since I was a little kid, and to hear poetry recited boldly, with emphasis and changes of tone and pace, was a revelation. (To this day, when I read Robert Browning, it's Keefe's gruff voice I hear. "Gr-r-r—there go, my heart's abhorrence! Water your damned flower-pots, do!")

And Keefe gave me another gift, almost by accident. I remember him saying—and I may very well have gotten it wrong, but if I did, it was exactly the right mistake— "Nobody really understands what the hell Hopkins was saying in 'The Windhover'. But it's beautiful."

On the one hand, this is complete nonsense. We know what Hopkins was getting at in "The Windhover" because he gives us a subtitle to tell us: "To Christ our Lord". His reflection on Christ in the image of the windhover, the beautiful falcon, is expressed in complex syntax and difficult, highly compressed language, but it's certainly an intelligible poem.

On the other hand, none of that mattered then. What mattered was that here was a poem that made my heart sing. I didn't understand it (no surprise: I was a raw eighteen-year-old, unused to poetry), but Professor Keefe gave me permission to love it anyway. Reading and responding to poetry without feeling obligated to break it down into nice tidy units of Theme and Meaning opened a door into a whole new world.

And Hopkins had a lot to show me.

Unlike Ellison, Hopkins offered a vision of the world that made sense even when life seemed arbitrary and confusing; his world had such things as justice and mercy even if one did not find them in one's own experience. Hopkins' world was integrated: it held pain, doubt, depression, and fear, but also joy and beauty and the sheer exultancy of being embodied.

Hopkins ends one of his most wrenching poems with a plea: "Mine, O thou Lord of life, send my roots rain." Will the dry spell end? Or will he continue to suffer? Hopkins doesn't know. He can only ask. His trust is deeper than his confidence.

Perhaps it was the integrity of his vision, his acknowledgment of both darkness and light, that made his words resonate with me, even though I had by this stage become consciously an atheist.

> There lives the dearest freshness deep down things;
> And though the last lights off the black West went
>   Oh, morning, at the brown brink eastward, springs—
> Because the Holy Ghost over the bent
>   World broods with warm breast and with ah! bright
>   wings.

The bumper-sticker expressions of Christian affirmation—
"I'm not perfect, just forgiven!" "God is my co-pilot!"—and
the kitsch art that I saw—a blue-eyed Jesus in drapey robes
(polyester?) comforting some repentant hipster, or cuddling
impossibly adorable children (none crying or distracted),
presented faith as a kind of pious flag-waving. "Look, I'm
Christian! I know Jesus!" Well, thanks, but no thanks; this
Jesus doesn't look like he could handle anything worse than
a skinned knee.

I didn't know then how to say it, but I was looking for
the cosmic Christ, the one by whom all things were made,
the risen and glorified Jesus at the right hand of the Father.

Hopkins' praise of God got past my allergic reaction to
kitsch because it flowed naturally out of what he saw in the
world. He let me step in and look through his eyes: I could
glimpse that "The world is charged with the grandeur of
God." In Hopkins' vision of the world, faith wasn't magic. It
didn't make ill health, estrangement from family, exhausting
work, and his poetry's failure into something he *enjoyed*.

Where his poetry was sweet, it had the sweetness of a perfectly ripe strawberry, or of the very best chocolate, creamy
and rich—not the chemical sweetness of a low-fat sugar-free
pudding with non-dairy whipped topping.

Where his poetry was bitter, it was bitter with the taste of
real misery, the kind that fills up your awareness, squeezes
out the memory of better times and draws a blank on tomorrow and tomorrow and tomorrow—not the faux-sadness of
"Jesus died for you!" (so cheer up and get with the program
already), the faux-compassion that can't bear to look at a crucifix (so morbid).

Somehow for Hopkins the sweet and the bitter were not
opposed; they were part of the same experience of being in
the world, and undergirding all of it was something I did

not understand at all, never having experienced it or known anyone who had: the reality of God, not as an abstract moral figure or as a name dropped to show off one's piety, but a dynamic awareness of being in relationship with the trinitarian God, an experienced reality bigger by far than the words used to point to it.

Hopkins' sense of the world was integrated because it was sacramental: something I would learn later on, when I discovered that the mystery of the Eucharist was the heart of my faith, the fount from which all else flowed.

But I didn't know, then, that I'd found something real; I let it slip through my fingers.

Intellectually, I had accepted a dis-enchanted view of the world. The beauty of nature was a side effect of the ceaseless, blind churning of natural selection; human culture was merely a product of clever animals with spare time on their hands. The glimpses of meaning from my childhood reading and the sheer exuberance and richness of my imaginative life seemed to have no bearing on my day-to-day experiences. There was no longer any space for transcendence in my life. Believing in God, and behaving as if God cared about what a puny human being might do, would be like acting out a fairy tale. No: imagination was one thing, and reality was another.

Nonetheless, I'd done something that secretly undermined the wall I'd built between my imaginative life and the 'real world'.

I'd become a fencer.

It would be hard to imagine a more unlikely athlete than I was at age seventeen. I was clumsy and slow, I was always picked last for teams, and in games I spent most of my time trying to stay out of the way of the other kids. Gym class was a demoralizing trial to be endured.

But the stories I loved were full of heroic sword-wielding knights and exciting battles. I admired Éowyn, Shield-Maid of Rohan, who brought down the leader of the Nazgûl in *The Lord of the Rings*, and thrilled to Kenneth Branagh's Saint Crispin's Day speech in *Henry V*. Sometimes, when I was washing the dishes (and nobody was around to see) I would pick up a carving knife and make flourishes with it, dispatching a villain or two before putting the clean knife away in the drawer.

Then, my first year at college, I saw a poster inviting new members to join the fencing club. No experience required. It was ludicrous to think I could be on a sports team. Still . . . fencing meant *swords!* I couldn't resist.

I showed up at the first practice and was put on the novice squad. It was a crazy, fun, eclectic group: even the 'jocks' were the kind of people who could quote chapter and verse of Monty Python. I delighted in fencing practice from the start, even when I was absolutely sure that the workouts were going to kill me.

I learned how to handle a foil; then, a sabre (it was love at first hit). I learned a new language: parry, riposte, en garde, advance, retreat, disengage, lunge, touché; I could name the parts of the weapon from pommel to tip, and I could take a sabre apart, replace a broken blade, and reassemble it. I discovered the pure joy of training eye, hand, body to work together in smooth unison to land a touch just-so.

What's more, I discovered that fencing had a code of honor and a hierarchy worthy of King Arthur's court. I learned that one must make a proper salute with one's sabre—neither too casual nor too florid—before each bout. It was natural to call the head coach 'sir': he seemed to combine the sagacity of Merlin with the derring-do of Sir Gawain. The team captains, like accomplished knights, shared their wisdom with us newbies on everything from how to make a feint-attack to how to stay hydrated during a tournament. And they regaled us with epic tales of road trips to National Championships and dramatic encounters with an archrival in the finals of a tournament.

Fencing wasn't like the books in many ways—the stories don't mention the Knights of the Round Table doing sit-ups and windsprints—but it was even better, because I was living it out. The reality of the sport fulfilled, rather than dispelled, the story-world enchantment that had attracted me to fencing. Imagination had proved to be a trustworthy guide.

Another seed had been planted, though it would lie dormant for years.

My fellow fencers were good company at practice and tournaments, but they never quite became part of my everyday life at college. Perhaps it was because I still didn't see myself as a 'real' athlete, or because I was the youngest member of the team; whatever the reason, I looked elsewhere for my social life.

I fell in with friends who were outspoken in their atheism and contempt for Christianity. I had nothing except a vague sense of wonder to hold up against this dismissal of purpose and meaning in the world; and I wanted a role to play that would let me fit in, in ways that I felt I couldn't as the bookish, overachieving, socially awkward young woman that I was.

In my twenties, my unreflective, copycat atheism gradually hardened into strident hostility. I spent two years of my graduate education in the South, where I was unhappy, in part because of culture shock: as a born and bred Yankee, I felt uncomfortable with the food, the weather, and the unintelligible accents of the locals. My exposure to Christianity did increase, but in forms that repelled me. A preacher would regularly come into the student quad during the lunch hour and rant about hellfire and damnation—at which point I would flee and eat my sandwich in depressed solitude in my library carrel. One time I was accosted on the way to class by an earnest hander-out of tracts: "Are y'all saved?" "No, and I don't want to be!" I shouted, half ashamed and half proud of being rude. Perhaps I could have met people of faith, but I was isolated and alienated, and I made no friends there.

I went back north for my doctorate, back to a safe and comfortable place. My dreadlocked, Birkenstock-wearing neighbors might smoke pot, burn incense, and enthuse about crystal vibrations, but I could be assured that nobody took faith, you know, *seriously*. Though I still understood next to nothing about Christianity, and cared less, I began to mock Christians and belittle their faith, their intelligence, their character.

I was not looking for God. Make no mistake: I did not believe he existed. I did not even wonder.

Chapter 6

WINTER AND SPRING

It was in fairy-stories that I first divined the potency of the words, and the wonder of the things, such as stone, and wood, and iron; tree and grass; house and fire; bread and wine.

—J. R. R. Tolkien, "On Fairy-Stories"

I wrote my doctoral dissertation on fantasy literature, with Tolkien's *The Lord of the Rings* as the center point of the argument.

This was a very peculiar thing for me to do.

I chose the topic of my dissertation precisely at the time that I consciously accepted and fully embraced the philosophy of atheism. And *The Lord of the Rings* is, in Tolkien's own words, "a fundamentally religious and Catholic work; unconsciously so at first, but consciously in the revision".

I was an atheist at odds with myself; I experienced a dissonance in my own life, in my understanding of the world. This dissonance was significant; it kept me from pulling the curtains on the outer world of grace completely. There was always a chink through which, irritatingly, a ray of light came to show the bleakness of my interior landscape.

And that light most often came by means of *The Lord of the Rings*, for Tolkien's world is one that is infused with grace.

It was a world in which the happy ending comes not in spite of suffering and brokenness, but through it: what Tolkien aptly named *eucatastrophe*, the good catastrophe, the unexpected turn after all hope is lost.

I cannot imagine any world more antithetical to the narrowness, the self-centeredness, the pointlessness of my atheist worldview, in which meaning is at best manufactured as an ever-less-effective opiate against despair.

I chose to do my dissertation on fantasy because I wanted to spend my time thinking about stories filled with marvels and strangeness, excitement and meaning, even if those stories had, as I thought, no bearing on reality. I focused on Tolkien, because—as I would have said then, just as I say now—*The Lord of the Rings* is the most important fictional work of the twentieth century. And so it happened that my topic immersed me in a sacramental world and brought me face-to-face with Tolkien's stirring proclamation of the *evangelium* in his essay "On Fairy-Stories". The hook had been set long since, and now the thread began to be drawn in.

Tolkien's story has a substance and heft that none of the many imitations has had. It feels real; it is imaginatively rich and nourishing. I realize now what I did not, then: it has the indefinable flavor of reality because it is somehow true, not historically, but spiritually and morally.

It is not intended as an allegory, nor should it be interpreted as one: insofar as there are Christ-figures in the book, it is because, as Hopkins puts it, "Christ plays in ten thousand places, / Lovely in limbs, and lovely in eyes not his / To the Father through the features of men's faces." In Aragorn, I first met the High King, the one who has been wandering the roads and fields, waiting for the time when he will come into his inheritance, a warrior with the hands of a healer. And as Lewis's Aslan would later show me what it meant for

God to become incarnate, Tolkien's Aragorn showed me a vision—which lay latent for many years in my mind—of the true king. Someone who deserved fealty, who inspired both awe and love, who could lead an army and tell a joke to put a friend at ease: the king who could walk among his people without being one whit less royal.

I didn't fully realize this connection until I reread *The Lord of the Rings* for about the eighth time, now as a Catholic, at which point the parallel between Aragorn and Christ the King seemed so vividly apparent that I thought to myself: How did I never notice this before?

I didn't know enough then to notice it . . . but I took it in.

By the spring of my thirty-first year, something had begun to change in my interior life. Like tree roots that slowly grow below sterile pavement, until one day the cement cracks and green shoots push up between the fractured bits of stone, the grace that had infused my imagination began to have a noticeable effect. I was drawn, against my own inclination, to be consciously interested in matters of faith. I had a desire to push into territory that I vaguely feared and yet found compelling.

I had started to read poetry again.

While getting my doctorate, I had become seriously burned out. For several years after I finished my degree, I worked in jobs outside my field, unsuccessfully casting around for some sense of purpose, some meaningful way to use the skills I knew I possessed. I tried my hand at creative writing, ending up with reams of half-finished stories shoved into my desk drawers and a lingering frustration with my own lack of direction. I watched a lot (and I mean a *lot*) of television. One thing I had *not* been doing was reading the poetry that I had fallen in love with as an undergraduate.

But now I was in California, with an unexpected fresh start, and I began teaching part-time at the college where I would be hired full-time the following year. I was excited to be back in the college classroom for the first time since graduate school, and teaching literature, not freshman composition. I dusted off my beloved *Norton Anthology of English Literature*, and, remembering what I'd learned from Professor Keefe and my other English professors (who had given me a far better education than I realized at the time), I turned to the canonical poets whom I had encountered as an undergraduate and now knew I needed to teach.

The greatest works of English literature spring from Christian roots. And so, atheist though I was, when I turned back to literature I found myself rereading poems of explicit and profound Christian faith. I rediscovered the work of T. S. Eliot, George Herbert, John Donne, Gerard Manley Hopkins, and the Anglo-Saxon poets whose names are lost to history. Consciously, I dismissed their faith as antiquated, or subjective, or irrelevant; I took the condescending view that their work was worth teaching *in spite of* this irritating fascination with God. But knowing a poem is experiential, like knowing a person. In order to teach a poem you must know it inside and out: its nuances, its shifts of tone, its images and their play upon the imagination. A great poem speaks more fully and deeply upon each reading of it.

And something happened as I read.

John Keats, in "Ode on a Grecian Urn", closes with these words: " 'Beauty is truth, truth beauty,'—that is all / Ye know on earth, and all ye need to know." Beauty: I had admired it, appreciated it, been moved by it, but until now had not thought deeply about why I responded as I did. Something had changed. I could feel power thrumming in the lines of the poems, an electricity of meaning, drawing from some source beyond my reach, and I began to wonder what that source was.

I read John Donne's "Holy Sonnet 14", and was drawn into it. I was deeply moved without knowing why. Intellectually, I recognized that Donne was Christian, and that I did not share his beliefs, and in fact I would have said that the God he addressed in the poem was imaginary and the faith he expressed was irrational nonsense.

Except that's not what I felt when I read and reread this intense, forceful poem. Donne speaks directly to God, offering a confession of weakness, pleading for him to break down the barriers of sin and pride:

> Batter my heart, three person'd God; for you
> As yet but knock, breathe, shine, and seek to mend;
> That I may rise and stand, o'erthrow me, and bend
> Your force, to break, blow, burn, and make me new.

Break, blow, burn, and make me new. Those words rang my heart like a bell. I did not believe as Donne believed, but I was powerfully stirred. *I, except you enthrall me, never shall be free* ... The words, once alien to me apart from my appreciation of their technical precision, now felt alive and potentially meaningful.

What Donne shares in this poem, the imaginative experience of a relationship with the living God, awoke longing in me. I would not have said, at that point, that I wanted his faith (because I had no reason at that point to believe that it was true) but for the first time I wanted to learn more. What was this 'faith'? Maybe it was something richer, deeper, more interesting than what I had always assumed.

I turned back to Gerard Manley Hopkins, hungry for something I couldn't name. "The world is charged with the grandeur of God. / It will flame out, like shining from shook foil." Hopkins blazed with intensity, illuminating a dimension to the world that I had not believed existed.

I had so carefully honed my defenses of denial, individualism, and rebellion, and here was Hopkins slipping past my guard:

> Not, I'll not, carrion comfort, Despair, not feast on
>   thee;
> Not untwist—slack they may be—these last strands
>   of man
> In me or, most weary, cry *I can no more*. I can:
> Can something, hope, wish day come, not choose
>   not to be.

It was a palpable hit. Hadn't I been feasting on Despair for years? And I was starving. I read and reread "Carrion Comfort". Hopkins spoke what I had never shared with anyone, what I had scarcely dared to admit. He had been where I was—and had not stayed there. *Hope, wish day come* ... Was there such a thing as day for me to hope for?

Hopkins was passionately, unashamedly Christian, but he did not blunt sharp edges. Here was no call to a comforting and trivial faith, no bland assurance that if I would come to Jesus I would feel better. Hopkins cries out to God:

> But ah, but O thou terrible, why wouldst thou rude
>   on me
> Thy wring-world right foot rock? lay a lionlimb
>   against me? scan
> With darksome devouring eyes my bruised bones?
>   and fan,
> O in turns of tempest, me heaped there; me frantic
>   to avoid thee and flee?

It was the winter of my soul. I had no conscious desire to find God; I thought I knew that he did not exist. And yet something was at work in me, just as Hopkins wrote in "The

Windhover": "My heart in hiding / Stirred for a bird...".
My heart stirred—for what? For something beyond my
experience.

Poetry had done its work. I was ready to listen. And the
person who would speak what I needed to hear would not be
a poet or a professor, nor even a pastor or a priest, but rather,
my fencing coach. Who would have thought?

Interlude 2

When I showed up to attend church at St. Michael's by-the-Sea for the first time, I was almost as skittish as if I'd still been an atheist: nervous, above all, about these *other Christians*.

I'd made my profession of faith barely two months earlier, and this was only the third time I'd been to church at all. St. Michael's was an Episcopal church in the high Anglican tradition, so it was very different from the big nondenominational Evangelical church where I'd attended a couple of services with my coach and his family. There were pews instead of chairs; the altar was front and center, with candles in tall, ornate candlesticks at the corners; stained-glass windows and tapestry wall-hangings depicted saints and angels. A great crucifix hung over the altar, a *Christus Rex* depicting the risen Christ as King.

The service involved lots of standing and kneeling and flipping between the service-sheet and the hymnal, but I managed well enough, and somehow it seemed right. The restrained, formal language of the liturgy felt both natural and fitting, and in reciting the prayers and responses along with the rest of the congregation, I was drawn into participation without feeling that I was putting myself forward. The whole service, indeed every part of the church, suggested a richness of meaning as yet beyond my grasp. I felt oddly at home, even though I was there by myself.

After the service, I could have fled through a side door—admittedly an attractive prospect—but I figured "in for a penny, in for a pound", and so I ventured to say hello to the deacon on the way out. So much for a discreet exit.

The deacon greeted me as if I belonged there, rather than as the stranger I was. Though I was startled by his warmth, it had such an unaffected quality that I was not put off by it. "Glad to meet you! Here, let me introduce you to Father Doran!"

Before I could say much of anything, I had been maneuvered through the line and neatly deposited in front of this young guy with a shaggy beard, dressed in black with a white priest's collar, just like in a BBC program, and *very* tall: the top of my head just about came to his shoulder height. That was my first impression of Father Doran, who would become my first pastor and spiritual director.

"Hey! Nice to meet you! I'm Father Doran! What brings you to St. Michael's?" He shook my hand enthusiastically.

I had never met a priest before. Somehow I didn't expect him to be so . . . *cheerful*. Later on, I would see time and again this quality of joy in other priests and deacons, expressed in different ways by different men, but at the time, I was taken aback. I managed to get out a few sentences of introduction, touching on the fact that I was not just new to St. Michael's but to this whole 'church' thing in general.

He was enthusiastic. "That's awesome! So, tell me your story! How did you become a Christian?"

And that was when he had me.

My experience had been that most people will ask a question to be polite. They do not really want to hear your answer; they just want to exchange a few pleasantries and move on. But as soon as Father Doran asked, I could see he genuinely wanted to hear my answer, and he actually listened to it.

A week or two later, I ran into him in the fruit and vegetable section at Trader Joe's. Even though he wasn't wearing his priest collar, I recognized the big bearded guy, and he recognized me. "Hey! How are you doing?" That quality of genuineness was there again: a smile and a nod would have sufficed for social purposes, but this priest, practically a stranger, actually cared how I was doing.

It seemed that maybe these Christians weren't so bad after all.

Chapter 7

INCHING FORWARD

Why, why dost thou hang back? why in thy breast
Harbour vile fear? why hast not courage there
And noble daring?

—Dante, *The Divine Comedy: Hell*

When I moved to San Diego I considered myself fortunate
to have found an excellent fencing club at which to train,
one with friendly, welcoming people who were also talented
fencers. I swiftly came to respect my new fencing coach,
Josh, as an intelligent, well-educated, and thoughtful person,
as a disciplined athlete and as a gifted teacher.

After almost a year of taking lessons, I found out, almost
by accident, that my coach was Christian.

I was surprised, to say the least. I had a lot of negative
stereotypes about Christians, and Josh didn't fit any of them.
By now, I knew he was genuine; I couldn't use my typical
explaining-away tricks for dismissing his faith. He was a caring and gentle person—though not a pushover—and there
was something different about him, something I had never
seen before: a kind of peace. His wife, Heidi, was also a fencer
at the club, and though she was very different from Josh in
some ways—she was much more outgoing, for instance—I
discovered that she had that same underlying joyfulness.

I liked these people. I enjoyed spending time with them. I wanted to be more like them.

And they were Christians!

It didn't match what I would have expected. Here I was, an atheist (which my coach figured out much more speedily than I figured out he was a Christian), yet Josh never reproached me for my unbelief, never tried to foist religious pamphlets on me or have an 'important conversation' to tell me how to be saved. Wasn't that what Christians did?

When I'd been in North Carolina for my master's degree, I'd encountered so-called 'friendship evangelism' for the first time … and formed an immediate and lasting aversion to it. During one of the 'welcome to campus' events, I ended up chatting with another young woman. "Some of us are having a picnic and a volleyball game this afternoon", she said. "We'd love for you to join us!"

Really? That sounded nice. I had been hoping to make some new friends. Perhaps these Southerners weren't as awful as I feared. We chatted a bit more. She was full of smiles as she added, "And we're really looking forward to sharing the good news about Jesus with you!"

What? I was appalled. Bait and switch! Needless to say, I did *not* go to the picnic or the volleyball game. I refused to be someone's pretend-friend so they could sell me Jesus, thank you very much.

But Josh wasn't trying to sell me on anything. He was simply being my coach, the best fencing coach I ever had. He cared about me, not as a potential convert, but as *me*, a unique individual, and he always, always treated me with respect. You can't fake respect when you train with someone three hours at a stretch, two evenings a week, plus weekend tournaments, for a whole year. If your honesty, patience, and compassion are a mask, it is sure to come off at some point when you're dealing with an argumentative, easily frustrated, excessively detail-oriented fencer. (That would be me.)

I didn't respect Christians. I respected Josh and Heidi ... who were Christians. Something didn't track. Might some of my ideas about Christians be wrong?

By itself, the discovery that my coach was a Christian was something I could have shrugged off. But something had woken up in me as I was rereading those poems that spoke so powerfully about the experience of knowing God. For the first time in my life, I consciously wanted to engage with questions of faith. My inclination to talk about these issues took coherent shape: my coach was a person I thought I might be able to talk to.

Embarrassingly, however, I discovered that I simply didn't know how to talk about 'religion' at all. If I wasn't being caustic, sarcastic, or condescending, I had only one other option in my repertoire, which was to be silent on the subject. One of my high school friends was Jewish, and I had noticed that she and her family took their faith seriously, at least to the extent of observing the Jewish holidays and having Bar Mitzvahs and Bat Mitzvahs for the children. I liked my friend's family and I would never have made a snarky remark about their faith, but I also never asked a question about it, not once in four years of high school. It would have seemed like prying into a personal subject that had nothing to do with me, like asking to look at their bank statements. Keeping silent was easy and comfortable; it maintained a suitable distance between me and potentially touchy subjects.

Now I wanted to close the distance. I began to inch forward, taking tiny, almost imperceptible steps toward a conversation about faith. I mentioned that I had recently watched the Robert De Niro film *The Mission* on DVD, and really enjoyed it. Josh agreed that it was a fine film, and added that he liked its theme of redemption.

Redemption ... that was a Christian word. It didn't offend me, but I also didn't know what to make of it. I didn't even know what kind of question I could ask to understand better what he meant by that word. It was as if my path was blocked by a door with no apparent knob or handle. I was intrigued to know what was on the other side of the door, but baffled about how to open it.

What opened it would be one of my worst fencing performances ever.

Chapter 8

PERFECT JUSTICE OR
PERFECT MERCY

Love bade me welcome: yet my soul drew back,
Guilty of dust and sin.

— George Herbert, "Love (3)"

It was early March, and I was in Reno, Nevada, for a Division II North American Cup fencing tournament: a big event for me.

I started the day feeling ready for a breakthrough performance. I was confident I would make it to the semifinals at least, and not-so-secretly I anticipated winning the whole thing. Let's just say things did not go as planned. I fenced abysmally in the first round of pools (as my coach succinctly, and factually, put it, "You did *everything* wrong"). Then, instead of starting my comeback in the direct-elimination round, I continued making one mistake after another and lost the very first bout. It was the end of the line for me: an ignominious end to my high hopes. My coach studiously ignored me until I stopped crying; when I had pulled myself together, we had our debriefing conversation, analyzing what had gone wrong and why. I was glum but I realized that if Josh was talking about what we would address in the next

series of lessons, at least it meant he wasn't going to kick me
to the curb for one bad performance.

Still, I felt deflated. Debrief completed, I slunk off to my
hotel room to change out of my fencing gear, tail between
my legs.

A couple of hours later, I wandered back down to the
venue and watched the women's sabre finals (where I'd
hoped to have been!). I ran into Josh and Heidi, and they
invited me to dinner. Their company was a welcome distraction from brooding over my disappointing performance, and
the conversation was sufficiently interesting to continue past
our meal, so we found a place to chat in the casino coffee
shop. Slot machines stood in ranks on either side, flashing
and jingling; the crowds ebbed and flowed around us. This
was Reno, where people gamble 24/7: late as it became, the
lights stayed on and no tired barista came to shoo us out. And
that was a good thing, because the three of us stayed there, in
conversation, for hours: talking about God.

If we'd been in a normal cafe that had to close up at nine
or ten P.M., we might never have gotten where we did in
our conversation. If I had done well in the tournament, we
would probably just have talked about fencing. However,
considering how disconsolate I was about my performance
that day, I was glad to talk about anything *but* fencing. Mov-
ies we'd seen. Favorite books. As it turned out, we were all
fans of C.S. Lewis's Chronicles of Narnia.

"I've read a little bit of Lewis's other stuff," I said, "I'm
really annoyed with him. He says Jesus is either a liar, a luna-
tic, or the Lord. But he's leaving out that we can respect
Jesus' teachings, without the religion part."

"Well," Josh said, "Actually ..."

And the conversation went on from there.

We talked about whether it was possible to know that
there was something beyond death. We talked about where

morality comes from. We talked about the idea of a First Cause, a Creator of the universe. At midnight my roommate called to see if I was OK, since I'm not the type to stay out late. I assured her I was fine, wished her a good night, and went back to the conversation.

I'd had interesting discussions before, but this one was different right from the start. I felt completely awake, alert, and more than a little nervous, as if I was handling dynamite. But then, I was, wasn't I? All my adult life, if I had discussed religion at all, it was to dismiss it as nonsense. Now I was asking serious questions—and genuinely listening to the answers. What made this conversation different?

At the time, I just knew that I felt *safe*. I knew that I was respected, that neither Josh nor Heidi would try to convert me, so I could let my guard down in a way I'd never dared to before.

They offered no Bible quotes. No sharing of how God had worked in their lives. No appeal to my happiness or peace of mind. What, then? Philosophy. Ideas. Dialogue.

The upshot was that, right there in that noisy casino coffee shop, I experienced a radical turnaround from my previous perspective on all things God-related. My non-belief in God was still intact, but I had discovered that 'faith' wasn't at all like I thought it was. It could be based on reason. It could be questioned, discussed, investigated.

I swiftly discovered that Josh knew what he was talking about: whenever I challenged a point, he had solid information and clear reasoning to back up what he'd said. Just as he respected me as an athlete by not permitting sloppy technique, in conversation he respected me as a thinker by not letting me get away with vague generalizations or unchallenged assumptions. That was refreshing. It was, in fact, the same kind of give-and-take as in my fencing lessons: he knew what I was capable of, and so he pushed me right to my

limits, but not past them. I had enough to work with that I
was not lost, yet was stretching myself past where I was really
comfortable.

(A fencing lesson, working on practicing strong attacks.
He's making me repeat the attack over and over again, with
corrections, till I get it right. My leg muscles are burning—
I'm gasping for breath—he pauses. Him: "Tired?" Me: (gasp)
"Yes" (gasp). Him: "Good. Back to work. On guard.")

As we wrestled with these ideas, Josh answered my questions: not the questions that an evangelist might think I *ought*
to have, but the ones I actually *did* have.

I wasn't interested in talking about Jesus as Savior: the
very idea of a divine savior assumed many things that I was
far from accepting—that God exists, that he is good, that
he interacts with mankind, that he could have a Son. No, I
needed to start at square one.

For me, the term 'God' was heavily loaded, so we used a
safer term, the neutral, philosophical 'First Cause', and began
with a basic question: can we even know, reasonably, that
there is a First Cause of the universe? I held to the belief
that the universe just 'happened'. I knew that I couldn't back
up that assertion, but I also thought that the religious take
was simply to assert the opposite. I say no God; you say God;
great, we're done.

Except that it seemed like Josh had some actual support
for his claim.

Sensing my interest, he laid out a few of the cosmological
arguments for the existence of God.

The mere thought of philosophical apologetics might cause
some people's eyes to glaze over. For me, it was like asking
for a mere glass of water and getting champagne instead. I
was stunned by the very concept that there were rational
arguments for the existence of God.

Never mind whether I agreed with the arguments or not, the simple fact that Josh said, "Let's reason this out" rather than "You have to take it on faith" made me want to keep talking.

What's more, these arguments made frighteningly good sense. I could see, even right there in that casino coffee shop in Reno, Nevada, that they made more sense than I wanted to admit.

Looking back, I realize how important it was that I was talking to an excellent teacher—a gift not limited to those who teach as a profession. Anybody can produce a statement and say, "Take it or leave it", but someone with the gift of teaching can open up an idea in new and compelling ways ... like using the metaphor of a coffee cup when talking about life after death!

The coffee cup came into play when I argued that there is no way of knowing if there is an afterlife or not: that when you're dead, you're dead and you don't get to come back and give a report. By way of illustration, I pushed my paper coffee cup into the center of the table. "Look," I said, "my cup has a lid on it. You can't tell by looking at it whether or not it has any coffee in it. I might *wish* it had coffee in it, but I don't *know*. The afterlife is like that: it may be there, or not, but there's just no way for me to know on this side." Hah! I thought I had it nailed.

Josh looked at the cup. "Do you trust me?" he asked.

When I had first started at the club, I'd noticed that his other students wore a mask but no jacket during their lessons. Even so, I'd insisted on wearing full protective gear in my lesson, just like in a competitive bout. After the first few months, though, I realized that my caution was unnecessary, and I quietly began emulating my fellow students. Now I took fencing lessons wearing a T-shirt, meaning that even in a high-speed, complex bladework drill, even in a realistic bout-simulation lesson, even if I made a mistake, I had complete trust that he would never, ever hit me.

"Yes, of course", I answered, puzzled.

"So if I showed you this cup and told you there was a nice, delicious, hot latte inside, you'd believe me? Without being able to look inside?"

I squirmed a bit, but I had to concede the point. "Well, yes, I would. But that's because I *know* you."

"Well," he said, "I know someone who has told me that there's a life after this one, and I trust him."

I know someone. I had never heard of Jesus spoken of like that. Matter-of-factly. I don't remember what I said in reply, if indeed I said anything at all. But in my mind's eye I can see that coffee cup sitting there. *I know someone, and I trust him.*

He left it at that; I'm sure he knew I was far from ready to consider that this someone might be a person I would meet one day. We moved on to other topics.

"If you could do something wrong that would benefit yourself, and you knew that no one would ever know about it, would you do it?"

"No, I wouldn't", I replied.

"Why not?"

I didn't know.

We'd been talking about the question of where morality comes from. I'd been arguing vehemently for morality as a social construct, useful for helping people get along with one another. But when I was confronted with that unanswerable "Why not?" I could see the logical consistency of the point Josh was making: that I had to be getting my moral sense from *somewhere*. Since I had a strong sense of right and wrong—even though I often didn't follow it—and I had no way to account for it objectively, should I at least consider that my sense of morality pointed toward a Being of absolute goodness, from whom my own moral sense derived?

Yes, I had to consider it.

One of the most interesting things about this conversation, as I look back on it, is that Josh never tried to 'close the deal' on me—not once. Having asked me questions that I couldn't answer, it would have been easy for him to move toward the 'endgame': to suggest that I adopt the beliefs that he would say *did* answer those questions. If he had, I would have shied off: discussion over, permanently. But he kept the conversation focused on ideas, not on my personal response to those ideas.

Even so, at one point I felt so uncomfortable with how my assumptions were being challenged that I started to retreat into a disingenuous relativism. "Well," I said, "you believe in this stuff, and if that works for you, great ..." I stopped. I could see from the look on Josh's face that I had offended him. He hadn't been bothered in the least when I had disagreed with him, but pulling out the relativism card was dismissive and disrespectful.

In an intuitive flash, I immediately regretted what I'd said. I hadn't really meant it; it had been a defensive reaction to questions that were getting hard for me to deal with. I said as much, Josh nodded in understanding, and we returned to the discussion. I was left with a searing glimpse of how essential honesty was to this conversation. I wanted to know what was true even if I didn't like it; I wanted to know the answers to these difficult questions more than I wanted peace of mind. And indeed, starting that night, I gave up peace of mind for a good long time: these new questions hinted at answers that were more than a little unsettling to my comfortable godless view of the world.

It was getting on toward two o'clock in the morning. I had just one more question I had to ask.

"OK," I said, "you believe in God. I don't. When I die, what do you think is going to happen to me?"

I'm not sure what prompted me to ask that question. I think I was pushing the limits a bit, seeing if I could provoke a response that would fit my stereotypes of Christians, since absolutely nothing of the night's conversation had been what I'd expected.

He said, "I'd rather not answer that question."

I was surprised, and I recognized that I was getting more respect than I probably deserved: he preferred to say nothing rather than water down his response to make it more palatable for me. Suddenly I genuinely did want to hear the answer. "No, really, I want to know what you think."

"Well," he said, "I believe that we will come before God in judgment, and he will give each person either perfect justice or perfect mercy."

I sat in silence thinking about this for a moment. Slowly, I said, "And you believe that it would be better for me to know enough, beforehand, to ask for perfect mercy?"

"Yes, I do."

And that was all he said. Perfect justice or perfect mercy. At that dim morning hour, and again as I thought about it later, I recognized something important: *I didn't want justice.* I considered myself a 'good person', but in my heart I was afraid to be judged on the real self behind my outward image. Perfect justice was terrifying ... and yet, completely fair. It wasn't that God would punish me for not believing in him. It was that he would dispense to me exactly what I deserved. Perfect justice.

Or perfect mercy. Not condescension, not humiliation, but mercy. I recognized that if there was a God, I would rather have mercy than justice.

It was still a big 'if'. But something in me resonated, like a tuning fork that vibrates long after it has been struck.

"I need to think about that some more", I said.

And I did. I'd intended to sleep on the plane on my flight home, but I couldn't. My mind and soul were too stirred up by what we'd talked about.

When I got home I wrote an e-mail to my coach. "Look what you've done!" I told him. These new ideas and their possible implications made me uncomfortable, but now that I'd admitted the questions as being real and worthwhile, I could not leave them unanswered.

I hit 'send'. I *had* to follow through.

Chapter 9

ON GUARD

He took his vorpal sword in hand:
Long time the manxome foe he sought—
So rested he by the Tumtum tree,
And stood awhile in thought.

And as in uffish thought he stood,
The Jabberwock, with eyes of flame,
Came whiffling through the tulgey wood,
And burbled as it came!

One, two! One, two! And through and through
The vorpal blade went snicker-snack!
He left it dead, and with its head
He went galumphing back.

—Lewis Carroll, "The Jabberwocky"

Given how adamantly I had held that faith, especially the Christian kind, was stupid nonsense, I found myself in an awkward situation when I recognized that there might actually be something to this God business. I now keenly wanted to pursue this line of thought, but I was ashamed and afraid to do so publicly. For years I had cultivated an image of myself as a tough intellectual who didn't brook any superstitious nonsense. I was proud of my ability to face meaninglessness without despair. Was I to lower my defenses, just like that? I wasn't sure that I could bear to let that image go and reveal the uncertain seeker behind the confident façade.

A few days after our conversation in Reno, my coach came up to me after practice and told me he had a couple of books he thought I would be interested in. One was *Does God Exist?* and the other was *Making Sense of the New Testament.* I took the books into my hands gingerly, as if I was handling explosives, and hurriedly tucked them away in my fencing bag to look at later.

I was aware that in order for me to consider these new ideas on their merits, I had to be ruthlessly honest with myself and with Josh when I talked with him. Could I trust him to respect my point of view, my questions? Could I count on him not to make me feel like an idiot? I was pretty sure I could, from what I knew of him. It still felt like a risk.

I began reading *Does God Exist* and taking notes.

Right away I realized I was onto something important. Peter Kreeft's introduction begins by posing the question "*Why* would someone want to prove that God exists? Why would someone want to prove that God does *not* exist?" and gives as one of the main reasons "simply for the sake of truth". I copied that into my notebook with an exclamation point. For the sake of truth! Here, it seemed, was someone who might just possibly be speaking a language I could understand.

When I got to the next page it was as though a great light flooded my mind. Kreeft writes that there are two kinds of thinkers, the tough-minded and the tender-minded:

> The 'tender-minded' on both sides [atheism and theism] would argue their case ... for happiness or goodness or utility or comfort or peace or 'needs' (usually a code word for *wants*)

or something of that kind. The 'tough-minded' put truth above even happiness. They want to know the truth whether or not they think it will help them to be happy.

Kreeft follows with a point that struck home even more:

> I think two tough-minded people could understand and respect each other better, even if one were an atheist and the other a theist, than either one could understand and respect and fruitfully argue with a tender-minded person, even if the tender-minded person shared the same belief about God.

When I pointed out this passage to Josh, he remarked, "I think I recognized early on that you were a tough-minded sort of person, the type it would be interesting to converse with."

I realized then that he wasn't just interested in winning me over to the Christian side but in the ideas themselves, and what I thought about them, regardless of whether I came to agree with him or not. That was reassuring ... and I needed some reassurance. I felt prickly and antagonistic, ready to lash out.

But Josh was no less poised as an apologist than he was as a fencer.

The easiest opponents are the ones who make big, flashy moves—impressive to the newbie, but not to the experienced fencer. You might lose a few early touches to someone like that, but as soon as you figure it out, all you have to do is step back, let the opponent fall short, and riposte swiftly and cleanly (most satisfyingly, to the head). Even better, if you can get a show-off to lose his temper it usually means an easy win. The really tough opponents are the ones who stay calm, don't over-reach in their attacks, and refuse to take the bait when you set up a feint-attack. That kind of fencer is also, by far, the most satisfying to fence with.

At practice, it was always a treat when Josh would set aside some time for his students to fence with him. Any touch that I managed to score was exciting because it was well-earned; the points I lost were helpful to show where my technique or tactics needed improvement. Sometimes, when Josh had scored the winning touch, he would say: "One more", and we would fence for another touch or two, just so that I could grasp what was happening and learn from it. The bout itself was intensely rewarding regardless of whether I won or lost, because of the sheer focused attention that it called for.

Being strong-willed (read: *stubborn*), I needed my intellectual sparring partner for discussion of the claims of 'faith' to be someone who wouldn't feel threatened when I disagreed; who had the humility to want to learn about my perspective, yet the authority to present the truth without caving in or glossing over the hard parts; who knew the difference between major and minor issues, and could firmly steer the discussion away from rabbit-trails. Josh fit the bill.

If I were brave enough to take up this challenge, the emphasis wouldn't be on the end result of declaring a winner or a loser, but on the experience of intellectually crossing swords. Just as in a fencing bout, how we approached this conversation—rigorously, courteously, thoughtfully—mattered a great deal. The discussion had a purpose, but the experience would be valuable in its own right.

If I were brave enough.

Chapter 10

CROSSING SWORDS

He looked vaguely about at the fire that was already fading, and there among the ashes lay two shining things that had survived the fire, his sword and Turnbull's, fallen haphazard in the pattern of a cross.

—G. K. Chesterton, *The Ball and the Cross*

The basic ideas from the Reno conversation were clear. Now I was considering them in the bright light of day. I'd had plenty of ideas that seemed brilliant at the time, but on reflection turned out to be castles in the air. I had an 'out' if I wanted to use it: I could dismiss the conversation as the product of a peculiar and fanciful mood, interesting but irrelevant to my 'real life'. I could let the conversation wither on the vine. After all, I didn't have to follow up; I didn't have to finish reading the books Josh had lent me.

Except that Josh had been presenting and defending his arguments with what I recognized as a keen intellect. If I dismissed the conversation as if it were equivalent to tipsy undergraduates philosophizing at a dorm bull session, then I would be making a deliberate falsification of the experience.

The part of me that I recognized as the best part of me—the part that held truth and honesty as absolute values, no matter how I sometimes failed to live up to them—would not let go. The argument for a Creator made sense: more sense, indeed, than my vague hand-waving that the universe had just 'happened'. If I didn't follow up to see if it was true or false, then I would be an intellectual coward, backing off from an idea because I feared it might be true.

Call me too tough-minded for that. Pen in hand, notebook at the ready, I set to reading with a vengeance.

In the introductory chapter of *Does God Exist?*, Kreeft wrote that "it is right and fair to explore and test faith by reason". I liked that. He then concisely outlined the pro and con arguments for the existence of God, noting that it is necessary to distinguish arguments against 'religion' from arguments for or against the existence of God. I liked that too. Methodically, I made a list in my notebook of the pro and con arguments he outlined: Cons: numbered (1) through (5). Pros: numbered (1) through ... (25)!

Before I had even gotten to the list, Kreeft had annihilated what I had thought was my ace in the hole argument against the existence of God: that humans had invented the idea of God for comfort, or out of fear, or to control people, or to explain what was inexplicable in the days before modern science. Indeed, Kreeft noted that "One of the atheist's strongest arguments has been his ability to explain the origin of the idea of God without a God." Aha! I thought. Refute that one! "But", Kreeft continued, "*when* is it reasonable for us to look for such psychological explanations for the origin of an idea? Only after we know, or think we know, that the idea is false. We don't give psychological explanations for the origin of the idea that $2 + 3 = 5$ or that the sun is round. Thus the Freudian argument begs the question. The God-question cannot be settled that way, psychologically."

Ouch. He was right; devising psychological or cultural just-so stories for the idea of God meant assuming ahead of time that the idea was untrue and therefore required outside explanation. As a scholar, I ought to have realized that the argument was fatally flawed; I had been blinded by my own assumption that God did not exist.

Chastened, I got out my notebook and set to work assessing, as best I could, each argument pro and con. Methodically I crossed out each item that seemed unconvincing and circled the ones that seemed to have merit.

The con list was short, but it seemed to cover all the bases. Regretfully, I crossed off several of the atheist arguments as implausible. I might not believe in God, but I did not think that the idea itself of God was logically self-contradictory— goodbye, no. (3)—and I rejected no. (5), "the negative consequences of belief in real life", as being just as irrelevant to the pursuit of truth as the positive consequences of belief. I found that I was unwilling actively to assert con no. (1), that the existence of evil disproves God; at most it would disprove a kindly God. Similarly, I didn't feel that no. (4), "it is not proved that God exists", was much of an argument; after all, I might not be able to prove mathematically that I, myself, really existed, but I was nonetheless quite sure that I did.

That left me with only no. (2), "the existence of God is not necessary to explain nature." I circled and starred it: my last, best hope for atheism?

Moving to the pro list, I began merrily scratching off one argument after another. I cared nothing for arguments based on mystical experiences, the reliability of the Bible, miracles, or the experiences of martyrs. So much for those! Hah! Then I hit a speed bump: I had to draw a circle around no. (10), "the existence of conscience: if there is an absolute moral law, there is an absolute moral lawgiver." I retaliated by vigorously double-x-ing out "the individual's need for the moral idea of perfection" and "the bad consequences of atheism". It might be bad for society if people didn't believe in God, but so what? Truth was what I was looking for, not rules for society.

I paused but could not in good conscience cross out the next item, "the eternity of truth leads to the existence of an eternal mind"; it seemed plausible. However, I hesitantly crossed out the "aesthetic" argument, that the beauty of art and music points to the existence of God. In retrospect, I ought to have circled it; my own response to story and poetry led in that direction. But it wasn't a connection I made at the time.

I happily crossed out nos. (15) and (16), "need for meaning in life" (I didn't need meaning!) and "Pascal's wager: your only chance of winning eternal happiness is believing, and your only chance of losing it is not believing" (having faith just in case there's an afterlife? I wanted nothing to do with that!).

I left alone no. (17), "C. S. Lewis's argument from desire: every desire corresponds to a real object, and there is an innate desire for God" as I didn't know what that argument was, but I respected Lewis enough to want to find out more. This gave me pause; I realized that I had been blithely dismissing arguments without first taking the trouble to understand them.

My x-ing became less confident. I crossed out nos. (18) and (19), the arguments for a Creator from the design of nature and the functioning of the human brain, but hesitantly, adding a question mark next to them.

When I came to the last quarter of the pro list I realized that I wasn't going to get off easily. I found myself unable to cross out any of the last six cosmological/philosophical arguments. Three of them I left unmarked, as I finally admitted that I couldn't assess what I didn't understand, but three I was forced to circle: the argument from motion to a first, unmoved mover; the existence of a First Cause; and the argument that time is meaningless if uncreated and infinite. This was heavy-duty philosophy, but having been introduced to the cosmological ideas in Reno, I knew they made enough sense that I wanted to learn the details.

When I was done, I reviewed my lists. I was perturbed by the result. I was left with four solid pro arguments that seemed very reasonable indeed, and several more that might be worthwhile. In contrast, I had almost nothing on the con side. If I was going to follow the guide of reason, it looked like reason wasn't going to accommodate my atheism easily.

I brought my notes and my questions to fencing practice, to see what Josh would say. His fencing student had suddenly become a philosophy student too.

Following up on these ideas was a seemingly small step, but a significant one. I had assumed that the existence of God was one of those things that you had to take on faith and that therefore any argument about it would be endless and circular, ending at best in agreeing to disagree. Now I was accepting the challenge of accepting or rejecting arguments based on reason rather than blind prejudice.

Many of the items that I had so intemperately scratched off the pro list could have been fruitful avenues for discussion with a bit more preparatory groundwork. The cosmological arguments attracted me the most perhaps because they were completely new to me, and so I could more easily approach them with an open mind. In any case, I was glad that Josh was willing to be a guide as I entered this strange new territory, rather than trying to choose the path for me.

We talked through the cosmological arguments for a bit. It was surprising to me that they were so clear and logical. I'd expected to find the arguments for God to be murky and mystical, full of holes that you were expected to leap over 'in faith'; in reality the arguments were anything but murky.

One of the key arguments had to do with causation. Josh presented what is known in philosophical circles as the Kalam cosmological argument: All things that began to exist had a cause; the universe began to exist; therefore, the universe had a cause. What could I make of that?

I had been content with the idea of our universe beginning with the Big Bang; the problem was that while I was eager to claim that science could not tell us what happened before the Big Bang, I was forced to admit that our lack of information did not preclude reasoning about what might have come before it. It was logical to ask, "If the Big Bang started it all off, what caused the Big Bang?" I knew it didn't work to assert that the universe had come, by natural forces, from nothing: if there were natural forces at work to generate the universe, that wasn't 'from nothing', but from 'something different than what we see now', which is not the same thing. It was easiest to take the universe (or the multiverse, which simply scales up the problem without changing it) as a brute fact, something that simply *is*. But then, just as with my own existence, I had the nagging sense that I was sweeping something under the rug. The origin of the cosmos had been on the list of Unknowable Things, and therefore offstage, not causing trouble with the way I understood the world.

Now it was causing trouble. Well, perhaps the chain of causality just went back infinitely, a cause behind a cause behind a cause, which would mean that there was no beginning to the universe after all. I wasn't terribly impressed by that argument, but I was curious to see whether there was a response to it. Did theists simply assert, "God did it"? Well, no. Josh patiently explained that it is impossible to have a beginningless universe, or a universe whose beginning is infinitely far in the past, because it is impossible to traverse an actual infinite. Since time involves the movement from one moment to the next, if there were an actual infinite number of moments, we would never be able to arrive at the present moment.

I knew when I was outflanked. All right: I agreed that the universe had a beginning. I agreed that, having had a beginning, the universe had a cause. And whatever this 'First Cause' was, it was itself uncaused: as Aristotle put it, an Unmoved Mover. Whatever-it-was that acted as the first cause had to be different from everything that came later.

What were the implications of that idea?

Here my coach brought in a line of thinking that at first seemed unrelated. He asked me to consider that there are different types of causes. "Imagine you have a cup of coffee on the table," he said, "and the cup falls over and spills. Why did it fall over? The table moved, but not by itself; something caused the table to move, maybe something bumping the table, maybe an earthquake. These are event-to-event causes; each event is part of a chain of causes and effects."

"I'm with you so far," I said. The coffee cup made such a useful metaphor. Where would it lead me this time?

"Now imagine you reach out and knock the cup over. You would be the cause of that cup being knocked over, without going any further. You have what's called personal agency, which means that you can be the 'first cause' of a chain of events."

"OK. So ...?"

"The point", he said, "is that the only kind of cause that could be a true First Cause is one that has personal agency: otherwise it couldn't be a true first cause and would instead just be one more link in a cause-and-effect chain of events. So the First Cause would have to be, in that sense, a Person."

He added, "This will make more sense when we look at it in conjunction with the other arguments for the existence of God."

Looking at this idea of a personal First Cause from different angles, I could not find any good reason to reject it.

Granted, if the universe were a completely closed system and I had no free will but was just responding as the environment and my genes necessitated, then the idea of personal agency was false. Certainly there were scientists who argued that freedom is an illusion, yet it seemed a delicious irony that they would write books as if the readers were free to agree or disagree, and act on the decision, and it was peculiar that the collection of genes that is 'me' would be capable of detecting and being amused by that irony.

My own experiences, my imaginative life, my aesthetic and emotional response to the world, stood against a purely determined, closed system.

It was possible that I did not actually have free will and personal agency, but only thought that I did; it was possible that I could not trust my own ability to reason. However, the fact that something is possible does not make it either likely or reasonable. The question is not: Can I come up with an alternative of any kind? but rather: Does this idea explain the data more effectively, more robustly, than the alternatives? The idea of a First Cause made very good sense.

I was almost frustrated with myself. I thought I would be putting up more of a fight than this. At the same time, though, I was intrigued, because I saw new vistas opening up in front of me. Since it appeared that there was, after all, a Creator to the universe, could we know more—could we know its character? More questions, and, I hoped, more answers, lay ahead.

Interlude 3

One day at the beginning of the fencing season I showed up in my priest's office with a prayer request. "This may sound strange," I said, "but I know you won't laugh at me. You know how important fencing is to me."

"Yes, I know", Father Doran said. Of course he did. He had prayed with me a number of times the previous year when I had badly injured my arm and didn't know if I would ever fence again, and he had given me a blessing on many occasions as I set off on trips to fencing tournaments.

I hesitated. Was my fencing truly important enough, or spiritual enough, to pray about? Then I remembered how often Father Doran had reminded me of Paul's injunction to "Pray without ceasing" (1 Thess 15:17). Whatever came up in my life, Father Doran said, pray about it! So I launched into my request. "The competitive season is about to begin," I said, "and I want to approach it differently this year. In the past I've gone into the season wanting to win tournaments, or get results that make my coach proud of me. This season I want to let all that go, and just fence my best for God's glory. I mean, I still want to do well, but I want to get my priorities straight, you know?"

He nodded in immediate and confident agreement. "Of course!" Father Doran said, taking me seriously as I had known he would. "Let's pray!"

So he traced the sign of the cross on my forehead, in the name of the Father, the Son, and the Holy Spirit, and laid his hand on my shoulder, and we prayed together to God who, among his many gifts and blessings in my life, had also given me the gift of fencing. I committed my competitive season to God, so that, whether I won or lost, my efforts would be for his honor and glory.

Ten months later, at the end of the season, we prayed together again, this time in thanksgiving. It had not been all victories: I had finished almost dead last in an important event in Portland, Oregon; in San Diego I had taken a wrenching second place in a regional tournament I'd badly wanted to win. But even in defeat, I found that I was able to let go of my disappointment in a way I never could before. Throughout the whole season, whether I was at a local meet or at a Division I North American Cup, I had been able to fence with joy, with my focus on doing my best rather than on winning, or on impressing my coach, or proving something to myself.

Unexpectedly, my season of prayer-for-fencing also brought new depth to my spiritual life. Over the months of training and tournaments, I found myself inclined to pray about other seemingly ordinary parts of my life, not just in the abstract but in the specifics: wrestling with the revision of a chapter, helping a struggling student, grading a stack of papers, finding time in a busy day to do laundry without grumbling.

"Pray without ceasing" had ceased to be an impossible bit of hyperbole; I had caught a glimpse of how prayer is part of an ongoing, beautifully mundane, day-in-day-out relationship with God. George Herbert, in his great poem on prayer, gave me words for the discovery: "Heaven in ordinary, man well dressed."

Chapter 11

SEARCHING FOR THE SOURCE

Teach me thy love to know;
That this new light, which now I see,
May both the work and workman show:
Then by a sun-beam I will climb to thee.

—George Herbert, "Matins"

It's hard to look at the truth when it runs contrary to what you've believed, even if you've been seeking a better understanding and you think you're prepared for new ideas. The experience is like finding a curtained window in a lamp-lit room, and curiously pulling back the curtains to get a view of the outside. If you are accustomed to artificial light, the bright sunlight is almost blinding, and causes your eyes to sting and water; when you turn away, even the room behind you seems darkened. The temptation is to pull the curtains closed, let your eyes readjust to the dimness, and return to using the more comfortable, controllable illumination of a lamp. Perhaps there is no sun, anyway: after all, what did you see except a bright, painful blur? But the electricity that powers artificial light is produced by fossil fuel, made from plants that long ago took in the light of the sun; or perhaps by solar panels, absorbing the sun's rays. We may think we are in control of the light when we can turn it on or off by a flick of a switch, but that tame indoor lamplight has its source in the wild heart of the sun, whether we realize it or not. The bright sunlight that at first reduces everything to a painful dazzle of white, and seems even to take away your power of sight, is precisely the light that makes it possible to see farther and more clearly.

It takes time for one's eyes to adjust . . .

I turned the idea of the First Cause this way and that way, turned it upside down, shook it, and it still held together. I tried to find a fatal flaw in the arguments, but at last I had to confess that I was convinced. At that point, to hold on to an atheistic or even an agnostic position would have been in defiance of logic and reason. All right: I accepted the existence of the philosophical First Cause, a unique Creator who brought the universe into being. This was not an emotional experience for me, unless a growing sense of discomfort counted as an emotion.

Now I was tempted to turn away from the window, to blink, and say "How interesting; the universe has a First Cause", and carry on with my life as usual. Except that what I'd glimpsed suggested a follow-up question that would require me to keep looking: What was this First Cause actually like? And did this First Cause have any interaction with human beings such as myself?

Looming very large here was the fact I believed that there is such a thing as good and evil. I held that there were such things as objective moral values. Somehow. Inconveniently.

At first I tried to weasel my way out of the implications of absolute morality by saying that values were useful but essentially arbitrary cultural constructions; we called things 'good' that benefited society, and 'evil' that harmed society.

Josh wouldn't allow me to have my easy escape: "In that case, why should you, yourself, be moral? Why not just do what is best for you, regardless of whether it hurts someone else?"

Well ... "If everyone did that, then society would break down", I argued.

He still wouldn't let me get away. "So? We're not talking about society; we're talking about you, personally, individually. If something would benefit you, why not do it?"

Here I could have asserted that I was culturally conditioned to think that certain things were good, except that I didn't actually believe that was true. I recognized that *some* of my behavior was culturally conditioned, like the idea that I ought to shave my legs if I was going to wear shorts; still, that did not mean that everything was conditioned or that I was incapable of distinguishing between the two. (We know that most mountain surfaces are formed by erosion, but we are still capable of recognizing Mount Rushmore as the work of human hands.) If our human capacity for reason was worth anything, it had to be able to see past the influence of culture, perhaps not always and not with absolute clarity, but at least partially, and as an academic I had made it my business to develop the capacity to do so. No, I could not in honesty respond that my moral values were rooted in nothing deeper than culture.

I could have argued that people hurt each other for their own profit all the time, but we weren't talking about other people, we were talking about me. I couldn't escape by generalizing. Would I harm someone to benefit myself, if I could get away with it?

Well, I might, after all. Who knows what I might do in a moment of weakness? But that just made the point more strongly, because even if I did, I would know that I was doing wrong. I could recall times that I had made excuses for neglecting a friend or when I had tried to convince myself that a somewhat shady course of action was actually just fine.

I remember once, as a student, being given too much change at the grocery store and noticing the error as I walked away. The question was: To give the money back or not? I remember arguing with myself and finally deciding to keep it, saying to myself, "I'm sure there are other times that I've been overcharged and didn't realize it, so this makes up for it." I had been too weak to resist the temptation of keeping a paltry couple of dollars, but I had known, though I tried to argue myself out of it, that I ought to have returned it.

As C. S. Lewis puts it in *Mere Christianity*, "If we do not believe in decent behavior, why should we be so anxious to make excuses for not having behaved decently?" Lewis continues:

> These, then, are the two points I wanted to make. First, that human beings, all over the earth, have this curious idea that they ought to behave in a certain way, and cannot really get rid of it. Secondly, that they do not in fact behave in that way. They know the Law of Nature; they break it. These two facts are the foundation of all clear thinking about ourselves and the universe we live in.

I had to be honest or this whole journey wasn't worth anything. I had to look at the evidence and concede that morality was not a human invention.

I remember the moment that I finally got it. Josh and I were standing outside the gym after fencing practice, talking about what the First Cause was like and where morality came from.

Josh said to me, "I bet that you are more certain of the fact that it is wrong to kill an innocent person than you are of the fact that there's a trash can right behind you."

I stood there and wrestled with the idea, resisting the urge to turn around and look behind me. I considered how certain

I was that there was a trash can directly behind me. There were a lot of trash cans, spaced evenly along the sidewalk in front of the gym; most likely there was one behind me. I couldn't remember if I'd seen it or not; trash cans are the kind of things that we look at without paying them any attention. *Probably* it was there ... but would I stake my life on whether there was in fact a trash can behind me? Definitely not.

On the other hand, would I stake my life on the truth that it is wrong to kill an innocent person? The answer was clear. Absolutely yes. I was more sure of this moral knowledge than I was of nearly anything else.

Frighteningly sure. Because that knowledge pointed outside myself. It was not something I needed to be taught; it was simply true. I could try to convince myself otherwise, but I knew certain things were good (kindness, honesty) and certain things were bad (murder, cruelty) in a way that was independent of myself.

What was the best explanation for this kind of moral knowledge? That there was an Ultimate Goodness, from which all virtues were derived, that transcended individuals and was beyond culture. Given that I accepted the existence of a First Cause, a Creator, on totally independent grounds, it was rational to conclude that the two were the same: that my innate sense of morality showed me something about the nature of the First Cause, that this Creator was also the source of all goodness.

I was looking for an explanation of the world that made rational sense. At this point, I had realized that my naturalistic framework was inadequate: it could not explain the origin of the universe, nor could it explain morality. On the other hand, the theistic framework for understanding reality was both consistent and powerfully explanatory: it offered a convincing, consistent, and logical explanation for everything that naturalism explained ... plus many things that the naturalistic view couldn't account for.

Josh began to explain a follow-up point: "In that case, we can see that the First Cause—"

I interrupted him. "It's all right, Josh. You can say 'God' now."

He laughed. "OK, then."

It was a small step, but one taken nonetheless.

Wherever it was we were headed, I was on the way.

Chapter 12

EXPERIMENT HOUSE

"I can't help wondering, can we—could we—?"
"Do you mean, do something to make it happen?"
Eustace nodded.
"You mean we might draw a circle on the ground—and write things in queer letters in it—and stand inside it and recite charms and spells?"
"Well," said Eustace after he had thought hard for a bit. "I believe that was the sort of thing I was thinking of, though I never did it. But now that it comes to the point, I've an idea that all those circles and things are rather rot. I don't think he'd like them. It would look as if we thought we could make him do things. But really, we can only ask him."
"Who is this person you keep on talking about?"
"They call him Aslan in That Place," said Eustace.

—C. S. Lewis, *The Silver Chair*

If it was true that I could pursue this journey as a rational endeavor, then why not do so with as much intellectual rigor as I could muster?

I had become convinced that the universe had a First Cause, a Creator, and that, rather than being an impersonal cause like one domino falling and knocking over the next one, the First Cause had intentionality, like the human being who chooses freely to reach out and tip over the first domino in the line.

What was more unsettling was my recognition of this First Cause as the being we could call God: the source of all morality. Now, if this was the case, then I thought it unlikely that God was an impersonal force simply pervading the universe like spiritual background radiation, leaving me alone to do whatever I wanted. God seemed capable of paying attention to great and small alike. Did the same First Cause who called the galaxies into being, whose word ignited the hearts of stars, also bend his attention toward me? Would this God from whom I had my sense of morality call me to account for what I had done and failed to do? If God truly was a Person, there were serious implications in my life.

In *Does God Exist?*, both Peter Kreeft and J. P. Moreland argued that a person could determine the truth of Christian theism, the Christian understanding of a personal God, by testing it out as applied to his own life. The idea of an experiment gripped me immediately. However, the two different approaches they suggested provoked radically different responses in me.

Kreeft suggested prayer: directly addressing this God whom I wasn't sure existed, asking him to let me know that he was real. My reaction was immediate and expressed in crude language; I surprised even myself with the intensity of my own response. I was still angry when I brought the idea up with Josh, and I emphatically repeated my reaction, obscenity included. To his credit, he wasn't put off by my choice of words, but read the situation rightly: as an indication that I had found myself unexpectedly in deeper waters than I could manage, and was flailing about as I sought to regain my footing. When I was arguing about an idea, he could (and would, and did) argue back and leave me with no escape from facing the idea's significance. This was different. He let me bluster for a bit and then shifted right back to discussing the topic on a more abstract level, where I felt able to consider the idea without feeling threatened.

I had rejected Kreeft's suggestion of prayer, but Moreland had suggested an alternative possibility. Although I'd been repelled by a passage in the book in which he'd referred to "fellowshipping with Jesus" (it felt too buddy-buddy), he had also mentioned that it was possible rationally to determine the truth of Christianity by testing it applied to your own life.

Could it be done? I was an academic, and a methodical thinker; I understood the concept of testing theories. The idea was to use a theory to generate predictions, and then check to see if those predictions were accurate; to the extent that the results matched (or didn't match) the predictions, you had supported or disproved your theory.

"Can we apply this to Christian theism?" I asked Josh. "I like this idea of testing things out. Moreland introduces the idea, but he doesn't follow it up, so you're stuck with it."

Josh was momentarily nonplussed. "Good question. You're challenging me to think about this in new ways."

I laughed. "Turnabout's fair play."

He was game to try it out. He warned me, though, that even though we were trying to be analytical, it wouldn't be quite the same as a scientific experiment, because the data would be experiential (feelings) rather than empirical (physical, measurable evidence). Fair enough. I appreciated the recognition that it wasn't going to be foolproof, and that the results might be inconclusive. I felt it was worth a try.

As I planned the 'experiment', loosely framed as testing the hypothesis that Christianity is true, I realized I had to get answers to some questions.

First, I asked, "What would be the predictions of this theory?"

He thought about it. "I think some would say that you would have an awareness of the Other. I would be more inclined to think of it as an 'I get it' moment, like when you see how a puzzle fits together."

That made a certain degree of sense, perhaps especially since it wasn't quite what I expected him to say. "OK," I said, "then what would disprove this theory, or at least force me to rethink it?" If there were no failure conditions, if any result could be interpreted as proving Christianity to be true, I would be sceptical of the value of the experiment. Josh suggested that 'failure' would be if I got nothing out of it or if I had feelings of increased confusion as a result. So far, so good: this experiment was evidently not rigged in favor of Christian theism.

Now we were getting into more difficult territory. "How will I be able to distinguish between wish fulfillment and genuine evidence, if the predictions are met?"

Josh was characteristically forthright. "That's the drawback."

I decided to try refining the idea. "Let's say the predictions are met. How can I know that it's because the theory is true? Maybe it would be just because the theory is a more effective ethical model." Josh argued that an ethical model that seemed more satisfying than what I had been able to come up with on my own would, in fact, count as evidence that it came from a higher reality; he reminded me that we weren't doing this experiment by itself but in conjunction with logical arguments, such as the argument for God from morality. I was willing to accept that.

I realized I had one more question, relating back to my difficulties with the concept of faith. "Can I expect a result at all if I undertake this as a test, or would I need to believe

ahead of time for it even to have a chance of working?" I felt
that a lot was riding on this last point.

Josh thought about that for a bit. "Another good question. Yes, I think you can genuinely do this as a test. Further, if you do it as a test and you get a result, I would
say that the result would be more valid, because it is less
likely to be influenced by 'wish fulfillment'. So a positive
result would be very positive. The question, then, is how
much weight to put on a negative result. Without sounding
like I am stacking the deck, I don't think a negative result
is all that determinative." He explained that if I didn't get a
result from my experiment, or if I got a negative result such
as confusion, the question would still be open: God might
still exist even if I did not experience him in a particular
circumstance.

I immediately made a connection to my experiences as a
teacher. Students often began class convinced that they were
'no good at writing'. My job was not just to teach them new
and more effective strategies for writing, but also to entice
them to give those strategies a fair trial. On many occasions
I had reminded my anxious students that one case of writer's
block didn't mean that the writing process I taught in class
was useless, and that an unsuccessful first (or second or third)
paper didn't mean they were doomed to failure in freshman
composition. Just so, I realized that in this case, if the experiment garnered no conclusive evidence (and I more than half
suspected that would be the case), it wouldn't necessarily
mean the theory was false.

OK, then; I asked, "You said you had several reasons for
saying that a negative result, or no result at all, would not
disprove the theory that the Christian idea of God is true.
What's the second reason?"

Josh put it simply: "He is not a tame lion."

I caught the reference immediately: the great lion Aslan, the Christ-figure in the Chronicles of Narnia. After the Pevensie children are crowned kings and queens of Narnia, Mr. Beaver warns them not to presume that Aslan will stay with them: "He doesn't like being tied down—and of course he has other countries to attend to. It's quite all right. He'll often drop in. Only you mustn't press him. He's wild, you know. Not like a *tame* lion."

A wild lion, met face-to-face—not mediated through a nature documentary on television, or kept safely distant by a fence at a zoo—would be both impressive and extremely dangerous. Indeed, in *The Silver Chair*, Jill Pole is terrified when she first encounters Aslan. "Do you eat girls?" she asks. The Lion is far from reassuring: "I have swallowed up girls and boys, women and men, kings and emperors, cities and realms."

Josh's allusion to Aslan was an abrupt reminder that the subject of my planned 'experiment' was a *Person* ... and a Person of infinite power, dangerous, unconstrained by what I would prefer 'God' to be like.

It was very nearly too much for me to take in.

My rejection of Kreeft's suggestion of 'talking to God' in prayer had not come from intellectual disagreement, but from a visceral reaction of fear and anger, and although the cause was new, the feeling of baffled rage was all too familiar. I had felt it when I was eight or nine years old, weeping over my long-division homework (and refusing to do it); in high school, my stomach in a knot as I stared at geometry proofs that meant nothing to me; as a college freshman, sick with frustration as I struggled with my chemistry problem sets. I knew that there was some meaning locked up in those figures, those equations and problems, but I was unable to see what the teacher (and the other students!) seemed to find so obvious, and my inability easily to understand made me both angry at myself and, eventually, dismissive of the subject.

The idea of a personal God was almost impossible for me to grasp to begin with, let alone the Christian claim that the Creator become a *human* person, flesh and blood like me, yet also fully God. The 'watchful dragons' (as Lewis calls them) of my rebellious self spoke up loud and clear, insisting, "It can't possibly be true that the Creator of the universe would respond to you, or even be aware of your existence. Who do you think you are, anyway? And these Christians are obviously talking nonsense. How could it be that the First Cause of the universe would somehow become a man, an actual human being walking around, getting his hands dirty, getting killed. Ridiculous. Who can believe that?"

I had nothing to say.

These new philosophical ideas about God made rational sense of the world as I saw it, but they did not show me that the God of the philosophers would have anything to do with me as an individual—much less that his concern for human beings would extend to becoming incarnate, as the Christians said that he had. God's morality might apply to me, yes, but like gravity, indiscriminately to all people; or like a law code, written down and handed over, with its authority coming from a distant Law-Giver. Surely he could not, would not, take notice of me: I was too small; he was too big. Surely he would not enter into his creation; it was grubby and messy and material, and he was spiritual and orderly and infinite.

I could understand the definition of the word 'Incarnation' but not grasp its meaning. It seemed unimaginable that God would come close enough to be touched, would become man.

Or was it? I began to recall glimpses of something I'd been intrigued by, yet had been unable to name, from an earlier, deeper vision.

What if the idea of the Incarnation did not have to be solved like a math problem ... what if I could get hold of its meaning in a different way?

I picked up *The Lion, the Witch and the Wardrobe*: this time, not to analyze it for my dissertation, but to enter Narnia like a little girl again.

And I encountered Aslan.

First just as a name, a glimpse of hope—"Aslan is on the move"—and then as a hope fulfilled, the great Lion really present in Narnia, bringing an end to a hundred years of winter. Aslan was a force to be reckoned with: he led the Narnians into battle, and killed the White Witch himself; when he roared, "they saw all the trees in front of him bend before the blast of his roaring as grass bends in a meadow before the wind." No tame lion, indeed.

And yet he was touchable, playful, personal. If I could have stepped through the wardrobe door and seen this character for myself, I don't know if I would have first run up and buried my hands and face in his shaggy mane, or fallen down before his great velveted paws with their terrible claws, afraid to look at him, but love and awe would have been mingled in both.

In Narnia, I found that the Incarnation was not a bizarre idea, out of place in the world. It infused the very atmosphere; I breathed it in and was strengthened by it. That God would join his creatures by becoming part of creation himself seemed, here in Narnia, as fitting as the fact that winter's end brought crocuses peeking brightly through half-melted snow; as right as the fact that sunlight warms chilled limbs and water quenches thirst.

In Narnia ... but here, in real life? It might not be true that God was involved with his world; it might not be likely that Jesus was God incarnate ... but it was no longer unimaginable. The experiment was worth doing.

Chapter 13

LIGHT FROM THE INVISIBLE LAMP

The others cast themselves down upon the fragrant grass, but
Frodo stood awhile still lost in wonder. It seemed to him
that he had stepped through a high window that looked on
a vanished world. A light was upon it for which his language
had no name.

—J. R. R. Tolkien, *The Lord of the Rings*

April in coastal San Diego. The winter rain had ended; the
weather was warming up; flowers burst forth in mad pro-
fusion. With May and June would come the seasonal cloud
cover known to locals as 'May gray' and 'June gloom', setting the stage for the hot sun of July, but before then came
bright, brilliant April. A few days before Easter, I was riding my bicycle home from work, pedaling slowly, thinking
once again about the questions that were occupying me. God
existed; what did that mean for me?

My route took me along the coast. The ocean lay to my
right, an expanse of blue dotted with surfers bobbing in the
swells; gulls careened overhead; an arrow-formation of peli-
cans glided majestically north.

Suddenly, and with a shock of recognition, I realized that
at a level deeper than I'd realized, I loved being alive. To be
sure, often I felt fractured, pulled in different directions, at

odds with myself ... but sometimes, I would feel a moment of glorious wholeness, a delight in simply being 'me' in a way that included my mind, emotions, body. Being outside on a crisp spring day: feeling sunlight on my face, hearing the crash and roar of waves, letting the breeze ruffle through my hair. Enjoying a good cup of coffee in the morning: the aroma as it brewed, the taste of the coffee, the warmth of the mug as I wrapped my hands around it. Most of all, fencing: not just the thrill of competition or the satisfaction of victory, but the wordless celebration of movement, the joy of being 'in the moment' with my body and my mind united in willed action.

Months later, reading Lewis's *Surprised by Joy*, I found the right words for what I had felt. Though Lewis and I each encountered this inarticulable joy for the first time in very different contexts—Lewis in reading stories, I in athletics—Lewis describes the shared experience with precision:

> [This experience of joy] is that of an unsatisfied desire which is itself more desirable than any other satisfaction.... considered only in its quality, it might almost equally well be called a particular kind of unhappiness or grief. But then it is a kind we want. I doubt whether anyone who has tasted it would ever, if both were in his power, exchange it for all the pleasures in the world. But then Joy is never in our power and pleasure often is.

The world was often painful to live in and difficult to understand, but every so often I got a glimpse of beauty at its core.

As I rolled to a stop at the intersection of the Coast Highway and Tamarack Street, I looked out over the curve of the coast and saw the dim outlines of the headland of La Jolla, with seagulls circling in the middle distance. For the very first time I considered eternal life as a real possibility.

The ground had fallen out from under my feet.

In our Reno conversation, though Josh and I had briefly discussed the idea of eternal life, it had been entirely abstract for me. As I'd told him then, the concept sounded appealing, but only in the same way that the idea of man being able to fly like birds was appealing. I could enjoy a fantasy story in which people could fly, and think "that would be fun if we could really do it", but all the while I would know as a basic fact that humans cannot soar through the sky on their own power. Knowing it to be simply fantasy, I could regard the idea of human flight dispassionately: a nice idea without any bearing on my own life.

I thought of Tolkien's Middle-earth, a world so richly satisfying to my imagination. What if I could go there in person? It would be wonderful to walk among the mallorn-trees of Lothlórien or have second breakfast in a hobbit-hole! I had never grieved over not being able to visit Middle-earth, simply because I'd always known that it was a place I could visit only in my imagination. But what if one day I learned it might be real? What if Rivendell could be found on a map, one that I'd always had on hand but overlooked, perhaps labeled with a different name?

Up till that moment, 'eternal life' had been no more than an abstract idea, unconnected to any of the desires of my own heart.

But if God was both real and personal, and if the claim that Josh so gently advanced was true, that the Creator could, and did, offer eternal life: what then?

I felt like I was waking from a long sleep, or emerging from numbness; as if something long-forgotten was coming back to mind. I looked at all the beauty around me and felt profoundly, deeply sad. It was impossible to grasp and hold the loveliness of this or any moment; it would always slip away through distraction and forgetfulness, fall apart into death and decay. My life was a brief candle; it would soon flicker and go out. I would die, and lose all that I loved so much.

Could it be true that God really does offer life that doesn't end? As I considered the merest chance that it really could be so, tears filled my eyes. The possibility of hope hurt like a blow to a hidden bruise.

I realized that now, if it turned out not to be true, I would no longer be indifferent: I would be angry, or sad, or both by turns.

As soon as I got the chance, I shared my experience with Josh. Somehow it was important for me to put it into words to another person, before I could explain it away or push it to the back of my mind.

For once, I didn't have a question for Josh; I had no argument to wrestle with, no intellectual problem to solve. Something had happened, and I simply had to reach out for some response, not knowing what was ahead. I had thought I was vulnerable before; I had not even guessed how much. Now I was acknowledging my own weakness, my own need, and no longer hiding behind the armor of atheist toughness.

It was a risk. Josh might have seized on this emotional moment as an opportunity to ask me to accept Jesus as my Savior so that I could enjoy eternal life. Shaken as I was, I would have felt any pressure as a betrayal.

Josh didn't push me to make a decision. He thanked me for sharing my thoughts and said, carefully, "I know you will anticipate my answer, and I assume you'll allow me to articulate it." And I did, because I trusted him.

He said, "This is the problem that I have heard explained as 'Why do we have a God-shaped hole in our beings?'

"We long for eternity in a finite world.

"We long for purpose, but life seems ultimately purposeless.

"We seem so incomplete.

"The theist says that God created us so that we could be completed in him. The atheist says that we create 'god' to fill the hole that was an unintended by-product of our evolution. What both sides agree on is that we have a hole ... an unfulfilled desire.

"How do we decide between the two? Does that 'hole' have meaning or is it accidental?"

And he directed my attention to something Lewis had written, in *Mere Christianity*, that spoke directly to my experience:

> Creatures are not born with desires unless satisfaction for those desires exists. A baby feels hunger: well, there is such a thing as food. A duckling wants to swim: well, there is such a thing as water. Men feel sexual desire: well, there is such a thing as sex. If I find in myself a desire which no experience in this world can satisfy, the most probable explanation is that I was made for another world.

Chapter 14

RESULTS

There comes a moment when the children who have been playing at burglars hush suddenly: was that a *real* footstep in the hall? There comes a moment when people who have been dabbling in religion ("Man's search for God"!) suddenly draw back. Supposing we really found Him? We never meant it to come to *that*! Worse still, supposing He had found us!

—C. S. Lewis, *Miracles*

Although I'd discussed the idea of the 'experiment' with Josh, I hadn't yet decided to begin it. I still wanted to work out some of the details, perhaps clarify in my own mind what I meant by the question "Is Christianity true?" and figure out what sort of result would answer it. I was beginning dimly to see that I was dealing with a Person, not some sort of impersonal spiritual machine, but somehow I still vaguely expected that nothing would happen until I chose to press the 'start' button.

A week or so later, I was once again coming down the Coast Highway, this time walking, taking the opportunity to reflect on these questions that had been occupying, in one way or another, a great deal of my waking attention.

I felt . . . odd. Different, somehow.

I realized, with a shock, that my experiment had started without me. And it had yielded results.

Of all the internal experiences I have attempted to describe in this book, this one is probably the most difficult. An atheist might dismiss it as 'all in my head'. Indeed, that is what I would have done in years past, if such a thing had been suggested to me as a possibility. A Christian who has had a relationship with God for a long time might take this kind of experience for granted, so that it doesn't seem like a big deal at all.

But for me it was completely new, utterly unexpected ... and uninvited.

What had happened was that I recognized a change in my internal state. It was like being feverish, while at the same time being completely well. Everything felt sharp-edged, preternaturally clear; as if the very rocks and trees and sky were poised to reveal some meaning beyond themselves. I felt the presence of something ... Someone ... that was within me, yet outside or beyond myself. With a feeling something like dread, and certainly like fear, I recognized what it was: an experience of the Other.

I had been wary of results that might confirm what I was looking for, so much so that I'd been deferring the question of what, exactly, I thought I might find if I were to look. And then, without my asking, I encountered the Other, God the Holy Spirit, in a way profoundly different from evaluating him as an idea. The question of wish fulfillment fell by the wayside.

Looking back, the experience makes sense in a way that it didn't, and couldn't, then. At that moment, I was still thinking through the philosophical issues, still trying to understand what the implications might be. Even though I would have conceded that in theory God could be encountered, I hadn't the least idea of what such an encounter might be *like*. The idea of 'knowing God personally' still seemed like a metaphor for a more advanced level of knowing *about* him.

I had accepted God as an idea; now, here, on the Coast Highway, I was confronted by a glimpse of his reality as a Person. And he made himself personally known to me in a way that I could recognize without being completely overwhelmed: in a way, perhaps, that might seem oddly anticlimactic to someone else. There were no visions, no voice, no tears: just a profound and inescapable recognition of the Other. Trust me, it was quite enough.

The fact that I recognized, beyond any reasonable doubt, that my 'experiment' had returned a shockingly positive result *before* I had consciously started it was the sting in the tail to this encounter. If I had known more what to expect, I might have accused myself of manufacturing my own results (disregarding the fact that it is the mark of a valid hypothesis when its predictions are fulfilled). If I had been actively seeking God when he came to meet me, I might have doubted the reality of the encounter, wondering if it was mere wish fulfillment and therefore to be disregarded.

But the what-ifs didn't matter in the end. I had my experimental data, and I could not ignore it even if I wanted to: not if I wanted to retain my own intellectual honesty. The experiment had not turned out as I'd expected, but it had produced results.

Now I knew something I had not known just a few weeks before: God was real and had landed a brief contact. In the privacy of my soul, an interior acknowledgment had to be made: "Touché!"

Interlude 4

The year after I became a Christian, I took a summer trip to England that included several days in Durham in the north of England. It was a kind of private pilgrimage for me, since N. T. Wright, whose book *The Resurrection of the Son of God* had been so influential in my path to faith, was at that time the Bishop of Durham.

The second day of my visit, I went to Matins at Durham Cathedral and was struck by noticing that the Diocese of the Rio Grande was included in that day's prayers for various churches and dioceses in the Anglican Communion. The reference was relevant to me because I had just the previous month been confirmed at St. Michael's by-the-Sea by the bishop of that very diocese, Bishop Steenson.

I was delighted to find a tiny link between the Cathedral and my home church, so as everyone filed out of the pews after Matins I went up to the priest to share that thought. As it turned out, he was the Dean of Durham Cathedral, and he seemed a kind and gracious man, so on impulse I asked if he would give me a blessing for the rest of my journey. He looked a little startled (perhaps he didn't get that request very often from American tourists) but readily acceded. He led me over to a side chapel (presumably so as not to get run over by tourists), laid his hand on my shoulder, and prayed briefly for me.

I haven't a clue what he said in his prayer (other than "In the name of God: Father, Son, and Holy Spirit") because as he prayed, the realization hit me: God was with me every bit as much here in England as in San Diego; in fact, he was closer to me than I was to myself, and so of course space and time could never take me farther away from him. This priest was a brother in Christ as much as my church family back home, even though I did not know him and would probably never see him again.

"I believe in the communion of saints ..." I repeated these words from the Apostles' Creed in the liturgy every Sunday; that moment in Durham Cathedral, I got a glimpse of what the doctrine *meant*.

It was not an abstract theological statement, but a description of reality: as if to say, "I believe in the ground under my feet."

What else was in the Creed whose meaning I had yet to grasp?

Chapter 15

BETWEEN TWO WORLDS

Broken in pieces all asunder,
Lord, hunt me not,
A thing forgot,
Once a poor creature, now a wonder,
A wonder tortur'd in the space
Betwixt this world and that of grace.

—George Herbert, "Affliction (4)"

Easter morning.

Something had fallen into place; I could feel it. I wrote a long e-mail to Josh. My hands were shaking as I typed, trying to get the words down and commit myself to the reality of the experience before I could convince myself it didn't matter:

> I think my heart has outpaced my head. It's as if the path sloped sharply downward, and I find myself going forward much more quickly than expected, pulled by a felt connection, like gravity. I say, "Wait! I need to reason this out!" but I'm already on the way—awkwardly and trying to slow down, but with a scary inevitability. Is this what it's like to get a little help from—well, I might as well say it—from Christ? Because it doesn't feel like I'm getting to do this at exactly my own pace, if you see what I mean.

99

This has been pretty scary. And still is, but for different reasons now, I think. If this isn't true—at the start I was afraid of being made a fool, of being guilty of wishful thinking, of trusting instincts that weren't trustworthy. I suppose I still am afraid of all those things, but at some point I have to trust something, and if I can't count on my own ability to figure things out and my intuition of what really matters, then I might as well give it all up. (Which is certainly an option. And an easier one in many ways, but I'd never be able to respect myself again if I bailed out that way.) But I'm also afraid now that if it isn't true, it will have been a cruel trick, to feel something that I think is real and have it taken away. I hope that's not the case.

And if what I feel is reliable, and real—that's scary too. I mean, if I thought it was tough at times just living up to my own standards of decent human behavior, with a world-view that says "Hey, that's just doing the best you can," then how tough is it going to be to have actual, genuine standards that are (literally) infinitely higher? But oddly enough, I almost feel like it would be easier, too, because there seems to be more of a point to trying. I often feel like I don't have my act together, that I could be doing so much better if I only knew how. I think that at this point, I would welcome a little help, if I could get it.

So my heart says, Yes, though my intellect says, wait, let us have more time for reason and evidence! I guess I just have to face up to feeling that way.

Josh wrote back:

I wanted to say something encouraging to you. Perhaps a quote ... I looked all over, in the Bible, in Lewis, but still feel concerned with saying something wrong (too strong, too weak) when you seem to be doing such a fine job of doing it right, of asking the right questions and finding the right answers, either from without or from within.

It is odd, I kind of know how to speak with people from a different kingdom than my own, I also know how to talk to people in the kingdom I belong to, I don't know quite what to say to you who are wandering in the countryside of the kingdom. It seems I should just let you enjoy the scenery. It speaks better than I could.

I do want you to decide to stay.

Chapter 16

HOLDING ON

O the mind, mind has mountains; cliffs of fall
Frightful, sheer, no-man-fathomed. Hold them cheap
May who ne'er hung there.

—Gerard Manley Hopkins,
"No Worst, there is None"

I found myself badly shaken by the recognition, that Easter morning, that I was past the point of mere intellectual assent. I had acknowledged that I had a Maker and that, as a result, I might have to reckon with Christ. What did it mean to live in the light of that knowledge?

I was fearless about heights as a child: able to look over steep cliffs and dare roller coasters without so much as a shiver. Not so now. Not long before, I had gone to Yosemite National Park and made my way to Taft Point. From a distance, I saw a pair of hikers seated on the rock outcropping, dangling their legs over the edge: an appealing image. It occurred to me that I might emulate them. I followed the trail up to the vista point at the cliff's edge and looked down into the Yosemite Valley. The view was breathtaking: sheer rock walls descended thousands of feet to the forest below, the river was a narrow sparkling ribbon between the trees, an eagle circled in the middle distance ... and there was only a token railing, nothing more than a wobbly frame of metal pipes, between me and that great abyss of empty air. My hands gripped the rail tightly, suddenly slick with sweat; my heart pounded; and I was considerably relieved when I stepped back a dozen feet to where I could have solid rock under my feet all around me.

I think the difference between my childhood fearlessness and my adult caution comes from a recognition of what it would mean to fall and the experience that accidents do happen. (I bear an inch-long scar on my leg from a mountain bike accident in college, when I tumbled half a dozen feet into a rocky streambed and gashed my shin open.) My adult imagination lets me vividly visualize the consequences if I were to slip, or if the railing were to give way, whereas to my childish self, danger was an abstract idea, something for other people to worry about.

My old moral sense was childish in that way. I sensed that yes, it was both possible and desirable to be better than I was, but I didn't know how to relate that recognition to my day-to-day actions. As I grew older, I developed a kind of practical morality: since I was the one who decided what was 'good enough' for me, I could adjust the demands of my conscience to fit the circumstances. Too-high expectations were unrealistic; what would be the point in setting myself up for certain failure?

Now, though, I found myself on a moral precipice, with the depths yawning beneath my feet and the heights opening up above me, nothing but thin air between me and the reality of the living God. Given that God exists and that he is the source of all that is good, then his goodness was literally infinitely greater than mine. Instead of being able comfortably to measure up to my own standards, I suddenly saw how utterly I would fall short—how indeed I did fall short—of the standards of the infinitely good God.

Moral vertigo.

Now it made sense why the world was both so beautiful and so broken: two pieces that I had never before been able to fit into the same puzzle. Beautiful, because the Creator, who is goodness himself, made it so; broken, because we in our pride (which I could feel in my own heart) turned away from him and made a mess of things. And because his goodness includes respect for us as individuals, he did not force us back into relationship with him, but instead allowed each of us, graciously, to come to him of our own choice, even while giving us the grace that enabled us to make that choice.

What would my choice be? I could feel the despairing appeal of being alone against an uncaring, meaningless world, the pride that would rather throw away all that is good, just to be able to say, "I am the captain of my soul."

Recognizing God as Creator and the Source of all goodness meant rethinking everything: nothing was exempt from that terrible scrutiny. Recognizing him meant admitting utter and complete failure to live up to the real standard of what is good.

In my heart I could feel the desire to pull the curtains closed, to block out this searing new light of understanding. I didn't know whether I'd be able to handle what I feared lay at the end of the road. What if I were mocked, condescended to, treated with disdain? I began to see how much I defined myself by what other people thought of me.

I told Josh, "If this goes where I think it is going, I'm not sure I'm going to be able to *tell* anybody." He laughed. "You're so *honest!*"

Faith, Lewis wrote in *Mere Christianity*, "is the art of holding on to things your reason has once accepted, in spite of your changing moods".

My mood was fearful, yes; but faith was no longer something alien to me. I knew so little, but what I knew, I could hold on to. I would not back out now. I could not.

Onward.

Chapter 17

ONE MIRACLE

In the Christian story God descends to re-ascend. He comes down; down from the heights of absolute being into time and space, down into humanity ... But He goes down to come up again and bring the whole ruined world up with Him.... One may think of a diver, first reducing himself to nakedness, then glancing in mid-air, then gone with a splash, vanished, rushing down through green and warm water into black and cold water, down through increasing pressure into the death-like region of ooze and slime and old decay; then up again, back to colour and light, his lungs almost bursting, till suddenly he breaks surface again, holding in his hand the dripping, precious thing that he went down to recover. He and it are both coloured now that they have come up into the light: down below, where it lay colourless in the dark, he lost his colour too.

—C. S. Lewis, *Miracles*

I had arrived at theism. I felt the attraction of getting comfortable with this brand-new belief in God, lingering in the realm of being spiritual-but-not-religious. Surely nobody could expect me to press onward immediately. Certainly Josh didn't. He was ready to let me take this at my own pace.

I could have dallied, but I felt drawn ahead, gently but insistently. It was as though I heard a tune, very faintly, that had been playing in the background for a long time and was only now becoming clear. I wanted to get closer, to hear the music completely.

Josh was a Christian; his rational faith had led him to believe that a man called Jesus of Nazareth was, in some strange way, the Son of God, the Savior. Could that be true? I conceded that it was at least possible. I had accepted rationally that God was One, that he was the Creator, and that he was the source of all goodness, as a result, many of the ideas that would otherwise have been attractive to me as a 'spiritual' person—paganism, Deism, pantheism—I recognized as being incomplete, or as contradicting what I'd come to accept as true about God. On the other hand, everything that I had learned, reasoned out, and experienced was at least compatible with the Christian conception of God.

I had acknowledged that God was real, and that in some way I had a relationship with him, but what did that mean? Did the Creator get involved in the muddy, day-to-day world that I lived in?

Right around this time, Josh lent me a book called *In Defense of Miracles*, a collection of academic essays that faced the question head-on: could miracles happen? I liked that the book gave space for the opposing view; it included a chapter by the well-regarded atheist philosopher Antony Flew as well as David Hume's classic essay arguing for the impossibility of miracles.

The question of miracles turned out to have practical implications. If the world had a divine Creator who remained hands-off, then large-scale changes in my naturalistic belief system would be unnecessary, and changes in my behavior would be somewhat less pressing. Nonetheless, the convenience factor of having my Maker be an absentee landlord didn't make it true.

As I read, I found that the arguments for the possibility of miracles were more convincing than the arguments against miracles. I had accepted God's existence on other grounds, and it was reasonable to conclude that the Creator was capable of interacting with his creation and quite likely interested in doing so.

But if I admitted that miracles could happen ... The implications made me dizzy. If God could act in the world any time, any place, did that mean that anything was possible? When I was a little kid, I had a rabbit's foot good-luck keychain; was I supposed to take stuff like that seriously? How could we even distinguish between the natural and the supernatural? For a moment, rational thought itself seemed in danger of becoming fuzzy.

When, a little panicky, I posed this question to Josh, he cut to the essentials. "Even with miracles being possible, we continue rationally to assess causes", he said. "We just have one more option for a cause."

As we discussed the concepts, I saw what he meant. My closed, naturalistic system was opening up: not to chaos and superstition, as I had feared, but to a more complex, more satisfying system, one that better explained my experiences of the world. In a closed system, it was difficult—in fact impossible—satisfactorily to account for things like the origin of the universe, the validity of moral intuition, free will, even the existence of the mind or the reliability of human reason. Formerly, I had ignored those questions, or accepted facile and unsatisfying answers, or started to follow the naturalistic explanations to their disturbing and ultimately amoral or immoral ends. Now I was free to step outside the box.

If natural reality was actually contained within a larger, supernatural dimension, undergirding and over-arching and thoroughly sustaining the world of natural causes—sometimes even intersecting with the physical world in ways that were noticeable by human beings—then what had puzzled me before now made sense. In particular, the experience of being 'me', a rational, thinking being who could make choices and exercise personal agency, made much more sense in this 'supernatural' understanding of the world.

The God who made the universe and from whom comes our moral sense cannot be a capricious or arbitrary God; by his very nature, he is order, reason, Logos. The natural world contains an infinitude of discoverable patterns and relationships, from the motions of the planets, to chemical reactions, to the life cycles of animals and plants; we apply our intelligence to the world around us and expect to be able to understand it more fully ... and we do. Even our ability to use language and have other people understand us—to write a symbol, or make a sound, and have a stranger in some other place or time understand our meaning—is a remarkable testament to the rational structure of reality.

And so, as I thought about it, I realized that even if reality included both the natural and the supernatural, it was still orderly, not a random flux of events.

It made sense that God could be involved in the world in and through natural causes, like a gardener pruning and watering selectively to guide the growth of plants already in the ground; but apparently Christians also believed God could work like an artist, painting new images directly and surprisingly onto the canvas of reality. There did not seem to be a sharp line between the natural and the supernatural the way that I expected. Properly understood, both evidenced divine activity—and the former was in fact a subset of the latter.

Yet *some* miracles seemed to stand out, to have an additional layer of meaning. In one sense, every sunset was a miracle—not least because of the remarkable human ability to appreciate its entirely useless and gratuitous beauty—but that didn't seem to be the kind of miracle that the writers of the Gospels were talking about. How could we tell which miracles we should pay attention to?

"This is how we would think about it", Josh said. "First, we would consider whether we had a good naturalistic explanation for something. Not just a possible one, but one that rationally makes sense. If not, we would consider whether there was a good reason to consider a supernatural explanation."

I saw that I had to let go of my old habit of thought, which was always to defer to any 'natural' explanation, no matter how far-fetched it might be. God was a Person, after all; he might choose to work behind the scenes, or in a more direct way. But I was still not sure how we could recognize direct divine intervention in the world.

Josh explained that we wouldn't call something a miracle just because we don't know how to explain it. Context mattered. For example, we don't know how to explain quantum events naturalistically, but, Josh said, "that doesn't mean we have to jump to calling it a 'miracle': rather, we would consider whether there was any reason to suspect more than merely natural divine action. We don't have a reason for that in the case of quantum particles, but there are other times when we do."

"Consider", he said, "the case of a man walking on water, who was verifying his divinity to followers who would soon go on to proclaim him to the world. In that case, we would have a good reason to think that water-walking was supernatural, rather than merely mysterious."

Quietly, then, that brought Jesus into the foreground.

I had been reading the Gospels. Jesus' ethical teachings were, in one sense, not very remarkable: they were rooted in the moral sense shared by human beings across cultures, what C. S. Lewis called the 'Tao'. Jesus might have expressed these precepts more clearly and forcefully than others had, but there was nothing in his teaching that particularly surprised or troubled me at that point (or that seemed to merit Jesus' execution as a troublemaker). Rather, what was unsettling was Jesus' claims—by word and action—about his identity.

He was a man who said, "Whoever has seen me, has seen the Father" (Jn 14:19) and "before Abraham was, I am" (Jn 8:58). He accepted worship; shockingly, he forgave other people's sins as only God could do (Mt 9). People marveled not so much that he taught and cast out demons, but that he did so by his direct authority (Mk 1:21–27). Jesus' divinity was a theme that was tightly woven into all the accounts of his life and teaching. Either the Gospels were sophisticated works of fiction in the modern realistic style, approximately seventeen hundred years ahead of the development of the genre—which as a literary scholar I knew was ludicrous—or the Gospel writers were describing what the man named Jesus of Nazareth had really said about himself.

Jesus' death and Resurrection began to loom larger in their significance.

A modern-day Lazarus might get a special on the Discovery Channel, but the day-to-day life of the world in general would not be changed by one ordinary man returning from the dead. People in the first century recognized a miracle when they saw one—they knew perfectly well that the dead, left to themselves, stay that way—but not all miracles carry the same meaning. The Gospels report several people being raised from the dead—a widow's son, a young girl, Lazarus— with no particular fanfare. Certainly their friends and family rejoiced, and the news spread, but nobody thought the miracle mattered much in a practical, permanent sense to anybody except their immediate circle.

However, Jesus of Nazareth was not just a man off the street who happened to get a second shot at life. The Christian claim, as I began to see, was not that Jesus was resuscitated, but that he was *resurrected*. He did not merely return from death to live out a regular human lifespan; rather, in going through death, he seemed to have done something to death itself, so that dying now meant—or could mean—something different. He had begun a new and different kind of life that the Gospel writers struggled to find adequate words to describe.

Jesus had talked about his death and predicted his Resurrection as if these events would have cosmic implications. Anybody could claim to be divine—the Roman emperors were getting in the habit of doing so—but Jesus went one crucial step further, and indicated how his claim would be put to the test. The Resurrection, if it happened, would be a vindication by God of Jesus' central, shocking assertion: that he was the Son of God, the Christ.

Jesus might or he might not have risen from the dead—I hadn't yet begun to investigate the question—but if he had, then the Resurrection was supremely meaningful.

I turned these thoughts over in my mind for a couple of days.

The Gospels were full of miracles. Had Jesus really walked on water? Had he fed five thousand people from just a couple of loaves of bread? When the sick came to him, did he really cure them with a word or a touch?

I could have spent a long time trying to come to terms with whether these miracles really happened, except that I saw, suddenly, that these were side paths, leading to interesting territory no doubt, but not going where I needed to go.

Not now. No more dallying in theism. I was ready to move on, to answer the bigger question. Was Jesus who he said he was?

There were many miracles that I could think about, but they all paled into insignificance next to the singular miracle of the Resurrection.

Had it really happened?

Because if it had, then Christianity was true.

Interlude 5

On that first trip to England, I also paid a visit to the Shrine of Our Lady of Walsingham in the county of Norfolk. The Shrine had come to my attention when I noticed that St Michael's by-the-Sea had, at a side altar, a replica of the famous Walsingham statue of Mary. A serene Mary, dressed as an Anglo-Saxon queen and carrying a lily, holds Jesus in her lap, and points to him; the infant Jesus, crowned as a king and holding the Gospels, raises his hand in a combined gesture of blessing to us and protection of his mother. Perhaps it was the combination of regal poise and familial tenderness in the depiction of both Mary and Jesus that caught my attention, or perhaps it was the connection to England; in any case, I was intrigued. Walsingham seemed a good place to explore.

Certainly the Shrine was rooted in Christian history, a thousand years of it. In 1061, the Lady Richeldis of Walsingham had a vision in which Mary showed her the house at Nazareth, the site of the Annunciation, and asked her to build a replica of it in England. This house became a place of pilgrimage and devotion, one of the greatest medieval English shrines, until it was utterly destroyed during the Reformation. After centuries of suppression, part of the Shrine, the Slipper Chapel, was restored in the late nineteenth century as a Catholic place of devotion; some decades later, a new replica of the Holy House was built nearby and became an Anglican pilgrimage site.

Getting there had been an adventure unto itself: I had heard it said, "No one gets to Walsingham by accident", and indeed that was the case. Oxford, my starting point, was flooded as a result of heavy summer rain, so instead of taking the (slightly) more direct route, I took a bus from Oxford to London, walked a couple of city blocks to the Victoria train station (glad my suitcase has wheels), caught a train from Victoria to King's Cross, transferred to a train from King's Cross to King's Lynn (wish my suitcase were lighter), navigated through several cross streets to find the bus station, took a bus from King's Lynn to the small town of Fakenham (why did I buy so many heavy books in Oxford?), and in Fakenham called the proprietor of the bed-and-breakfast where I was staying, who graciously picked me up at the bus station in a tiny little car where I sat, unnerved at riding along on apparently the wrong! side! of the road! as we drove to the even tinier town of Walsingham, where, finally, I could settle in.

I attended several worship services at the Anglican Shrine church during the first day of my visit. After the evening service was done, I lingered. Inside the main church were many smaller side chapels. I found one dedicated to the Risen Christ and knew immediately that this was where I wanted to pray. I lit a candle and placed it in the votive rack. Kneeling uncomfortably on the stone floor, I tried to lift up my confused thoughts to God. I wanted to write: I felt compelled to put down in words something of this Christian journey that was the most exciting and also the most terrifying experience I could imagine. Yet I was struggling with questions about my own motivations. Was it presumptuous that I should publicly tell my story? Was I doing it for the right reasons?

And I was anxious about life as a Christian, a whole life ahead of me in which God was now first and foremost. What would God call me to do? How would I know?

I don't know how long I stayed at prayer in that tiny chapel—long enough for my legs to get stiff and my knees to ache. As I looked at the votive candle, flickering in the dimness, I realized what that image represented. I could trust in Christ, the Light of the World. I didn't need to see far ahead, only far enough to take the next step forward.

If I had known what was ahead, I would probably not have believed it anyway.

The church in Houston, Texas where I would be received as a Catholic a few years later was (I am not making this up) dedicated to ... Our Lady of Walsingham. And remember Bishop Steenson, of the Diocese of the Rio Grande?

When I was preparing to be received and confirmed as a Catholic, the rector of Our Lady of Walsingham mentioned that "Monsignor Steenson" would be doing the confirmations.

"Wait," I said, "I know that name. Steenson,... is he by any chance a former Episcopalian?"

It turns out that Monsignor Steenson was indeed the former Bishop of the Rio Grande ... he had 'crossed the Tiber' not long after performing the confirmations at St. Michael's by-the-Sea. And so, five years later at Our Lady of Walsingham in Houston, he confirmed me for the *second* time—this time as a Catholic.

Truth is sometimes stranger than fiction.

Chapter 18

BODY AND SOUL

[I]n all that toil, that coil, since (seems) I kissed the rod,
Hand rather, my heart lo! lapped strength, stole joy, would
laugh, cheer.
Cheer whom though? The hero whose heaven-handling
flung me, foot trod
Me? or me that fought him? O which one? is it each one?
That night, that year
Of now done darkness I wretch lay wrestling with (my God!)
my God.

—Gerard Manley Hopkins, "Carrion Comfort"

I had once thought that Christianity was a soft, wish-fulfillment religion. Now I saw that it was entirely the opposite. Christianity made hard-edged claims about reality, about events in history, about who God is and how he acts. My search for truth had proved capable of leading to a rational faith in God. I did not have to leave the claims of Christianity in the no-man's-land of "I wonder if". The question was: Had the Resurrection really happened, not in a vague, symbolic, 'spiritual' sense, but as a fact of history? I might not be able to find out the answer; maybe it was something Christians just took on faith; maybe I would be stuck not being able to decide. But any way I sliced it, I had to try.

"All right, Josh," I said, "I want to read more—a lot more—about the historicity of the Resurrection. As scholarly as you've got."

At the next fencing practice, he handed over what I'd asked for. Two books. One was short: Gary Habermas's *The Risen Jesus and Future Hope*. The other was a massive tome. "You asked for scholarly", Josh said, handing me N. T. Wright's *The Resurrection of the Son of God*. No kidding! It was at least two inches thick.

I started in on the smaller book first. I had a fencing tournament that weekend up in Santa Cruz so I brought it to read on the plane. Now, just doing that made me feel a bit uncomfortable. Only a few weeks before, I'd been a card-carrying atheist professor, and here I was sitting in the window seat of a plane, reading a book with the word JESUS in big letters on the cover.

So, of course, it caught the attention of the woman in the seat next to me. "Oh," she said chirpily, "that looks like a good book!"

Oh, great. I don't like talking to strangers on planes; I just wanted to read my book. "Yes, it's a good book." (Hint: Let me read my book in peace!)

Hint not taken. She persisted. "So, are you born again?"

"No." Belatedly, I realized I was being unnecessarily curt, so I added by way of explanation, "I'm basically a theist, sort of agnostic about Christianity, doing some exploration."

"Oh."

The conversation having mercifully dropped stone dead, I continued reading.

In any case, the book was engrossing enough to make me forget being embarrassed by the cover. Habermas laid out a case for the Resurrection based on facts accepted by even sceptical scholars. Most of these facts were uncontroversial by themselves; the real question was what explanation could account for all the facts—not just one or two—in the most logical and coherent way? I needed to do more research, but at the least, his argument torpedoed my assumption about Christians just accepting it on faith.

If Jesus had not physically, bodily risen from the dead—if this thing called the Resurrection were just a spiritual experience in the hearts of Christians—then I could take it or leave it ... and I would leave it. As a purely subjective, internal experience, it would be of no interest to me. But Habermas provided a very plausible argument that the Resurrection had really happened. Was that argument solid? It looked like it, but I needed to push as hard as I could. When I got home from my trip, I rolled up my sleeves and started the next phase of my research.

Time for Wright's book. More than seven hundred pages. Small print. Hundreds of footnotes and a thirty-five-page bibliography with references in multiple languages.

I'd no sooner read the first chapter, in which Wright takes almost thirty pages carefully to define the multiple meanings of the terms 'history', 'death', and 'resurrection', and to present his approach for determining what really happened on the first Easter, when I realized I'd found someone who truly spoke my language. I saw that Wright knew his subject inside and out, that he was a deep and powerful thinker who could also express himself with clarity, and that he was relentless in his pursuit of accuracy and precision in the interpretation of evidence. My academic heart warmed.

I worked through Wright's book, notebook at hand, following up on questions with other research. If some scholars held that the Resurrection was a metaphor, or an emotional experience later recounted as if it was history, while others held that it was indeed a real, historical event, then only one of the two perspectives was correct; they couldn't both be true. Although just a few short months earlier, I would have assumed that the 'metaphor' view was (of course!) the correct one, now I had to let go of such comforting certainty.

Bit by bit, with painstaking attention to the details of language, culture, history, Wright built up an overwhelming cumulative case. When the early Christians spoke of 'resurrection', they meant bodily resurrection, not something purely spiritual. The earliest Christian documents—which, I discovered in my other research, are so early as to include eyewitness accounts—indicate that from the very beginning, the followers of Jesus believed that Jesus had been physically raised from the dead, vindicating his claims and inaugurating the new Kingdom of God, which would include their own future bodily resurrection. So, Wright asks, what is the best explanation for this belief?

What, indeed?

After hundreds of pages of painstaking analysis of the evidence, it was impossible to ignore certain facts.

Jesus was brutally tortured to death, in a way that under any normal circumstances would have marked his cause as a complete failure. His friends abandoned him. His dead, battered body was taken down from the Cross and laid to rest. But—the tomb was found empty. Even the enemies of Christianity admitted it. Then something else extraordinary happened: the disciples, singly and in groups, met the risen Jesus. The evidence was so clear that even the sceptics conceded that some kind of encounters had happened, which left them straining for psychological explanations that I could see did not adequately explain what had happened.

It was not enough to posit that the Church had in later years created a backstory of Jesus' divinity and Resurrection to account for belief in him as God. For one thing,

I'd studied oral tradition as part of my academic training; I knew what time frame and conditions were necessary for legend formation, and those conditions didn't hold here. Even if I accepted the most conservative estimates about the manuscripts' dates, the appearance of the Gospels and the Epistles did not provide enough time—not by a wide margin—for a legendary tradition to have developed about a divine Jesus before the events of his life and death were recorded

But more importantly, the suggestion that the Church had produced its own origin-story ignored a very large elephant in the room: the existence of the Church in the first place. In just a few short years after the death of Jesus, the Christian faith spread rapidly through the known world. From the earliest days, believers formed communities centered on the worship of Jesus, with eucharistic celebrations that caused rumors of cannibalism to spread among their pagan neighbors. How had this started? If the Church was not the result of a miracle, it was itself a miracle.

Something extraordinary had most definitely happened. The disciples went in short order from being fearful, cowering wrecks to bold proclaimers of Jesus, even though it cost many of them their lives. Paul, persecutor of the earliest Christians, an educated, zealous, energetic man (I liked him already), met the risen Lord and made a 180 degree turn from archenemy to apostle.

The apostles preached the crucified and risen Christ at a time when most of the eyewitnesses were "still alive" (1 Cor 15:6). And Paul followed up the implications bluntly enough: "if Christ has not been raised, then our preaching is in vain and your faith is in vain" (1 Cor 15:14). He knew what it would mean for himself and for all the other new Christians if the Resurrection had not actually happened. Implicitly, he challenged listeners to follow up and check on the truth of what he said about Jesus.

How could all this be accounted for?

In his quiet, scholarly way, Wright put the answer in front of me: the best explanation for the early Christian belief that Jesus had been raised from the dead was that it really happened that way.

I read through the Gospel narratives again, trying to take in what they said. I had to admit that—even apart from everything else I had learned—I recognized that they were historical narratives. I'd been steeped in folklore, fantasy, legend, and myth ever since I was a child, and had studied these literary genres as an adult; I knew their cadences, their flavor, their rhythm. None of these stylistic fingerprints appeared in the New Testament books that I was reading. In Paul's letters, I heard the strong, clear voice of a distinctive personality speaking of what he'd seen and heard and done. The Gospels had the ineffable texture of history, with all the odd clarity of detail that comes when the author is recounting something so huge that even as he tells it, he doesn't see all the implications. The testimony of women would undermine the credibility of these accounts in a male-dominated culture, and yet we hear of Mary Magdalen bringing the news of the risen Jesus to the rest of the disciples: the 'apostle to the apostles'.

Details are telling. And of all the odd details, the account of Jesus eating the broiled fish after his Resurrection struck me the most. If the disciples wanted to make up a story about their encounter with the risen Lord, surely they would have come up with something different. They might have invited him to their meal—that would be very symbolically pleasing! Or they might have omitted the food part entirely, to focus on the great spiritual insight they were receiving.

But that's not what the evangelist records. The disciples are confused and amazed. Nobody thinks to offer Jesus so much as a drink of water. He has to ask. That makes them look bad ... One can imagine the disciples, seized by embarrassment, casting their eyes over the disarray of the supper dishes. They offer him a piece of fish, and he eats it, and they have another confirmation that this truly is the Resurrected Lord: no vision eats a piece of fish. What a muddled, awkward scene! How much more convenient it would have been to tidy up the narrative, make it more impressive. The only reason to include an embarrassing scene like this would be that it was the way it happened.

The sheer physicality of the Resurrection stopped me in my tracks. I'm not sure what I expected, but not this. I suppose I imagined something purely 'spiritual', maybe ghostly, but definitely not bodily. At least I was in good company: the disciples were taken aback, too, when they saw Jesus for the first time.

Jesus had not been an inspiring idea. He had been a man, with flesh and bones. He had been a living, breathing, human with a beating heart, just like me. He had been put to death and laid in the tomb: his flesh cold, his heart stilled.

And then, when Jesus appeared to his terrified, cowardly disciples, he did so not as a spirit, not as a memory, but in his body. Here was the same Jesus who had been laid in the tomb—with the very same body, since the tomb was empty—and yet he was in some inexpressible way different. He was glorified, yet at the same time utterly physical, his flesh still bearing the marks of the nails. That struck me as something no one expected, something no one would ever have invented if it were not true.

I felt like this was ringing something deep within me. If this was true, if Jesus really did rise bodily from the dead, then it meant that he truly was the Son of God, the Lord.

And also—the Gospels and the Letters said it straight out—what was true of Jesus would also be true of those who followed him. Like his Resurrection, the eternal life he offered was physical and embodied. Forget about metaphorical 'life' in the renewal of nature or in the memory of my friends; in the end, those were just empty platitudes. Here was a sharp-edged promise that I would not die, but live; and that this new life would be as myself, individually and personally.

Until now, I'd never thought about what the word 'resurrection' meant. I'd thought that Christians believed in a vague 'life in heaven' as a disembodied spirit, which was not a terribly attractive prospect. But this! This was different, and it rang true. God, who had created me, had given me a body. Why do that, if it was just going to get thrown away? The pieces fit together. What he had made, he would renew. If what Jesus promised was true (could it possibly be true?), it made sense of the world.

I stretched out my hands in front of me and looked at them. Though I often thought of myself just in terms of my mind—after all, I spent so much of my time reading, writing, studying, thinking—in recent years as I had become a more disciplined athlete, I had discovered a deeper sense of self. The moments of greatest joy that I had experienced had been when I was fencing at full capacity, when my body and mind worked together perfectly in tandem.

If the Resurrection had really happened, it meant that my experience of being me, of being body and soul in deep connection, was profoundly validated ... and would be eternal. Or could be—if I accepted him.

Yet what was the price? What would he ask of me? And would it be more than I was able, or willing, to give?

Chapter 19

TAKING A DANGEROUS STEP

"Are you not thirsty?" said the Lion.
"I'm *dying* of thirst," said Jill.
"Then drink," said the Lion ...
"Will you promise not to—do anything to me, if I do
come?" said Jill.
"I make no promise," said the Lion.

—C. S. Lewis, *The Silver Chair*

A decision was necessary. It loomed like a thundercloud on
the horizon. I had to decide what the Resurrection meant, in
practice, in my own life.

The question was not what I wanted, but rather: "Is this
the way the world works?"

I was afraid. I remember one conversation, standing
around after fencing practice, following up on a question
about morality, finding that my hands were shaking uncon-
trollably. I swiftly stuck my hands in my pockets, determined
not to betray my anxieties quite so obviously. I don't know
if Josh noticed how nervous I was. Probably he did, because
he offered me a Bible verse to think about. Not a comforting
one, in the conventional sense. He quoted Psalm 111: "The
fear of the Lord is the beginning of wisdom."

This fear: it meant that I was starting to see more clearly.

I had been reading Lewis's *Mere Christianity* and feeling a deep affinity with Lewis. He was an English professor, an adult convert from atheism to Christianity, an author of fantasy literature. I knew I had to listen when Lewis spoke plainly about Christian commitment:

> Christ says 'Give me All. I don't want so much of your time and so much of your money and so much of your work: I want You.... Hand over the whole natural self, all the desires which you think innocent as well as the ones you think wicked—the whole outfit. I will give you a new self instead. In fact, I will give you Myself: my own will shall become yours.' ... The process will be long and in parts very painful, but that is what we are in for. Nothing less. He meant what He said.

This was not a God I could bargain with. It was all or nothing.

The first half of Gary Habermas's *The Risen Jesus and Future Hope* focused on arguments for the historical reality of the Resurrection, and N. T. Wright's scholarly work backed up those arguments in exhaustive and engrossing detail. But the second half of Habermas's book caught me by surprise. It addressed the consequences of the truth of the Resurrection, something I had not really thought about yet.

I told Josh that I was faced with a new idea. "If I come to see that the Resurrection was a genuine historical event—as I'm thinking is likely to be the case—what does that mean for me?"

He said simply, "That is the big question."

I continued to think about the implications. Between Habermas and Lewis, there was no way of escaping the recognition that, if I assented to the truth of Christianity, a truly radical commitment was required, which ran counter to what, formerly, I'd thought Christians believed. I told Josh that this 'commitment' idea was nothing whatsoever like the 'accept Jesus and be sure you'll get into heaven' idea that I'd heard many times.

"That's the problem of cheap grace", he said. "Some people treat Christianity as fire insurance, and that's not the way it should be." He acknowledged that God made demands on people, that God could call people beyond what they were comfortable with, or thought they wanted.

"Well ... look, Habermas talks about eternal life, and he also talks about Christ's expectations for people who accept him. This 'radical commitment' that seems to be required ... it's really frightening. I keep thinking, 'What would I be getting myself into?'"

Josh nodded. "I'm glad you feel that way. That is how it should be approached."

"And the other thing is ... isn't this promise of eternal life too good to be true?"

"Almost."

Almost ...

What would the Resurrection mean for me? What would happen to me? I felt that I was stepping out into darkness, fast approaching a point of no return. "My reason, my intellect have taken me a lot further than I ever anticipated. But how much further can they take me?" Struggling, I shifted back into the language of hypotheticals. "If ... if this all turns out to be true, is there another step I'll need to take, without using reason?"

"Yes, there is another step, and it is a fundamentally different step. But it is not without reason."

He continued, "The metaphor I like is of aviation. Let's say you are afraid to fly because you are afraid the plane will crash. I could sit and explain to you about aerodynamics and plane construction, step-by-step, until you are intellectually convinced that planes can safely fly. I could show you an airplane's logbook that shows it has been checked and signed off as safe to fly. You could even say that you believe that if you got on the airplane you would make it to your destination. It's a different step for you, yourself, actually to get on board that airplane and go on the flight."

I thought about it. "Will I know how to do it, to make that step, if it comes to that?"

"You will."

Josh's quiet assurance spoke more than any number of reasoned arguments or encouraging Bible verses would have. How could he have such confidence in me, when I didn't have it in myself? Still ... it was something to hang on to.

Chapter 20

FOUNDER

Enough! the Resurrection,
A heart's clarion! Away, grief's gasping, joyless days,
    dejection.
            Across my foundering deck shone
A beacon, an eternal beam. Flesh fade, and mortal trash
Fall to the residuary worm; world's wildfire, leave but ash:
            In a flash, at a trumpet crash,
I am all at once what Christ is, since he was what I am, and
This Jack, joke, poor potsherd, patch, matchwood, immortal
    diamond,
            Is immortal diamond.

— Gerard Manley Hopkins, "That Nature is a Heraclitean
        Fire and of the comfort of the Resurrection"

I had read all that I could read; more would do me no good.
I had worked through the arguments sufficiently; I knew
where I stood. It was a fact of history that Jesus died on the
cross and was raised on the third day, vindicating his claim
to be the Son of God. It was true. I felt strangely calm, as if I
were at the eye of some internal storm.

All the forces within me lay quiet, but in tension; I knew
that I could not stay in this place. Decision was required.

I found myself returning to the airplane metaphor. It captured how I felt about this step, this irrevocable step, that lay

somewhere ahead. You didn't just get on a plane after all:
you first bought a ticket, and that itself was a kind of commitment; and then you checked your luggage, and that was a
kind of commitment; and then you went through the secu-
rity checkpoint, and that, too, was a kind of commitment.
Even then, though, you could still turn back, wend your
way past the X-ray machines and the signs declaring "NO
RETURN TO THE GATE AFTER THIS POINT".

Where was the decision point?

Buying the ticket was not the same thing as getting on the
plane, but when you bought the ticket, by implication you
were announcing your intention. No more price-checking
online. No more trying out different dates on the calendar
or considering alternate destinations. You might be scared to
fly, but if you bought the ticket you were declaring that your
will had won out over your fears.

Yes, there would be the final moment of choice: get on
the plane, boarding pass in hand, or ... not. Maybe when
you got to the gate, you would be scared to board. But then,
what if you had someone there, someone to hold out a hand
if you stumbled as you made your way down the gangway,
someone to reassure you of what you already knew: that the
pilot was to be trusted?

A crucial decision point was buying the ticket.

Josh was confident that I could do what I needed to do.
But could I? And what would it mean if I did go forward? I
wrestled with the idea, back and forth, unsure, drawn, unsure.

Hesitantly, edging closer to decision without having made
a decision, I asked Josh, "Let's say I'm going to buy that
ticket. What, exactly, would I be getting myself into?"

He didn't answer at all how I expected. "Jesus says a couple of paradoxical things relating to this question", he replied.
"He says, 'Come to me, all who labor and are heavy laden,

and I will give you rest. Take my yoke upon you, and learn from me, for I am gentle and lowly in heart, and you will find rest for your souls. For my yoke is easy, and my burden is light' (Mt 11:28–30).

"But later, he says, 'If anyone would come after me, let him deny himself and take up his cross and follow me. For whoever would save his life will lose it, but whoever loses his life for my sake will find it' (Mt 16:24–25).

"I'll let you ponder that."

What kind of an answer was that?

It told me that the Christian life wasn't something to be figured out, like a philosophical crossword puzzle, but a reality to be experienced. This Jesus, whom I had dared to begin to believe had really been raised from the dead, said, "Follow me."

My options were clear; there was no more uncertainty.

I could choose to turn my back, to reject Jesus, and in so doing reject utterly God himself. Pride urged me to do it. This was the voice that whispered: "If you surrender, you lose. Be your own self, no one else's. Be a rebel."

Or I could accept defeat, lay down my arms, and acknowledge Jesus as Lord ... whatever that entailed. I knew the territory behind me; though it would be bitter to return to it now, the darkness remained seductive in its familiarity. What lay ahead in this second choice was unknown; it required trust, vulnerability.

I knew too much, and knew myself too well, to fool myself into thinking there was a middle ground. Jesus said: *Follow me.* I had to give him all, or nothing. Attempting to avoid making a decision would, in itself, be choosing to reject him.

And yet, I felt that I was in a space in between. I had reached a crossroads, yes, but I had been given a chance to pause for a moment, to really look the choice in the eye and know what was presented to me. I was uncertain about a great many things, but one thing I felt sure of was that I was free to choose.

I knew it was true that Jesus was the Son of God. I wanted to choose him, but something was in the way. I felt caught in a kind of inertia. There were countless questions I could ask, many subjects that I wanted to know more about, but to research more, at this point, would be a form of escapism: learning about God and Jesus and the Church so as to avoid confronting their living reality.

I opened my journal and flipped through the pages of notes, quotes, questions. At the end were several passages I had copied out from N. T. Wright's book. It felt as though he was speaking directly to my situation:

> There are various levels of self-involving statements. If, walking down the street, I say 'I think that was the Number 10 bus,' the statement is only minimally self-involving; I do not want to go where the Number 10 bus goes, and anyway I prefer to walk. But if, arriving breathless at the bus-stop on the way to a vital appointment, I look despairingly up the street and say 'I think that was the Number 10 bus,' knowing that the next one is not due for another two hours and that there is no other means of arriving on time, the statement not only involves me, it plunges me into gloom. The point is that one cannot say 'Jesus of Nazareth was bodily raised from the dead' with the minimal involvement of the first of those statements. If it happened, it matters. The world is a different place from what it would be if it did not happen.

No. I could not back away from making a decision. Slowly I reread one particular passage:

> Saying that 'Jesus of Nazareth was bodily raised from the dead' is not only a self-*involving* statement; it is a self-*committing*

statement, going beyond a reordering of one's private world into various levels of commitment to work out the implications. We cannot simply leave a flag stuck on a hill somewhere and sail back home to safety.

I was self-involved; what, then?

I set aside my journal. It was late Thursday night; the next day I had to catch a flight to Las Vegas to fence in the regional championships. I had to get some rest. I crawled into bed and fell deeply asleep.

I dreamed.

In my dream, Josh and I were walking in Jerusalem, and he was pointing out the sights to me. He was Virgil to my Dante, my guide and interpreter. Even in the dream itself I recognized that in some strange way I was acting out the *Divine Comedy*.

In the dream, we sat down on a bench across from a cluster of small stone buildings, gray in a dusty brown landscape. Josh, as Virgil, pointed to one of the buildings and said, "That's Jesus' tomb." We sat and watched the crowds of tourists coming to pay homage to the tomb where Jesus lay.

Then, in the dream itself, everything came together, and I knew, not just understood but knew, that Jesus of Nazareth is the Son of the living God. In the dream, I realized the falsity of the scene before me. After Easter morning, the tomb didn't matter. And why not? Because what happened that day was so big, so shattering, that it overshadowed everything else. The tomb was important only because they had laid the body of Jesus in it—and because on the third day it was *empty*.

The tomb was empty. *He is not here.* Everything clicked together, came sharply into focus, and in the dream my heart leaped with joy and I woke up. *He is risen.*

I lay there, in some small, quiet hour of the morning, abruptly and completely awake. The dream did not fade but stayed sharp and complete in my memory. For some time I had acknowledged that the only rational explanation of the events of the first Easter was that Jesus had indeed risen from the dead, without quite being able to accept it. In my dream, with my defenses all the way down (for when are we more unguarded than when asleep?), I could look with open eyes and open heart at the scene—and I suspect that in my dream, that tomb of Jesus with the tourists passing to and from stood for the whole argument, not just that one piece of evidence—and recognize what was in front of me and say: He is risen. It is the truth.

And something else. As I lay there in the dark, marveling at this new, complete thing that I had before me, I understood why I had been hesitating. I had been unwilling to say "Your will be done, not mine." I was afraid to let go of control, to abdicate authority over my own life and heart and will.

It turned out that buying the ticket was not the main thing. Nor was it handing over the boarding pass at the gate. Nor was it even stepping onto the plane and finding my seat. The main thing would be when the engines started and the pilot guided the plane off the ground.

At the very moment that I confronted my own fear, I knew that I was no longer bound by it. I was afraid, but I had made my decision. I would lay down my arms.

Chapter 21

CROSSING THE THRESHOLD

At one particular corner of the gooseberry patch, the change came.

What awaited her there was serious to the degree of sorrow and beyond. There was no form nor sound. The mould under the bushes, the moss on the path, and the little brick border, were not visibly changed. But they were changed. A boundary had been crossed. She had come into a world, or into a Person, or into the presence of a Person. Something expectant, patient, inexorable, met her with no veil or protection between.

—C. S. Lewis, *That Hideous Strength*

I had made a decision, but I had yet to act on it. It never even occurred to me that I could act on my decision right then, by myself. Mostly, that was because I simply had no idea what one was supposed to *do* with a decision like that ... but perhaps it was also because, at some level, I felt that a commitment made spontaneously and privately was no commitment at all.

The next day I traveled to Las Vegas, checked into the hotel, had dinner with another women's sabre fencer who was sharing the hotel room with me. I was still in-between, but I no longer felt strange. I knew I would see my coach there, and that he would help me make this last step onto the plane.

Saturday, I fenced. After the competition: time for hungry fencers to get some dinner. I met up with Josh and Heidi, one of their sons, and another of my teammates, and our little group set out on foot on the road leading to the Strip. It was hot, with Vegas' dry baking heat, and bright, and dusty.

"Let me tell you something", I said to Josh, and so we walked ahead a little bit.

"I bought the ticket", I said.

I glanced sidelong and saw his expression very briefly: a flash of almost-disbelief turning into a startled joy.

I recounted my dream, and what I had realized, and had decided to do. In the utter ordinariness of hungry fencers trudging along to go get food, it ought to have seemed odd or out of place to talk about Christ, but it didn't. It seemed the most natural thing in the world.

"There's someone we need to tell about this", Josh said.

"Who?" I was a bit confused.

"God", he said, drily.

"Oh. Right . . ." Now I felt out of my league again. "How do we do that?"

"We'll pray together. How about after we come back from dinner, we'll sit down together and we'll pray then?"

"OK."

We walked in silence for a few minutes. The paved sidewalk ended and we picked our way carefully over loose stones, passing in front of a vacant lot where construction was in progress. Abruptly Josh said, "Can I tell everyone about this?"

"What, right now?"

"Yes."

"Here?" We were on a street in the middle of Las Vegas and he didn't want to wait till the next day, or even the next hour, to share this news?

"Yes, right here!"

I daresay it's the only time I'd ever seen Josh impatient, but with a kind of happy impatience. Awkward as I felt, how could I say no?

So we stopped, and in a pace or two the rest of the group caught up with us, and Josh said, "I have some great news. Holly has decided to become a Christian!"

And I got congratulations and hugs and cheerful words of "Welcome to the family!" and now as a whole group, we kept walking toward the Strip, chatting about fencing and the day's results and books we had read recently. That was my first Christian fellowship: among people I already knew, liked, and respected as coaches and teammates and friends.

We arrived, finally, at the Strip, and decided to go for a buffet dinner inside one of the big casinos, the one with the Eiffel Tower on it. We filled our plates, declaring sincere intentions to go back for seconds to the dessert section, and came back to our table and sat down. Then Josh said to me: "You're part of the family now, Holly, so since we're all Christians here, we're going to pray." So he said a blessing over the food, and we set to our meal.

It struck me: *This is how we do things in the Kingdom.* With belief came action, even in small things.

After we returned from dinner, Josh and I sat down in the garden outside the fencing venue. He spoke briefly about what it meant that Jesus had died and risen from death for us and asked whether I wanted to pray with him out loud or in silence. "Out loud", I said, "because I need to say the words, to be sure I'm really doing this."

So he prayed, and I repeated his words, acknowledging Jesus as my Lord and Savior, recognizing that I was a sinner in need of salvation, committing myself to God, and asking for a personal relationship with Jesus. And that was the first time, in my whole life, that I said a prayer.

We sat for a moment in silence. I felt slightly limp, as if I could sit there indefinitely. Josh, being more practical, got up and bade me a good night. Right: I had to fence again the next day. Life did go on. "Good night", I replied, and walked slowly back to my hotel room.

Did my roommate notice anything different, as she and I exchanged pleasantries about our hopes for the next day's fencing? Probably not. Everything was different, but I sensed that it was going to take a while to figure out what, exactly, that meant in practice. Everything seemed both supernaturally charged and completely ordinary at the same time.

Changes surely lay ahead, but what would they be? Lewis had been very direct about how much happened *after* conversion: "You must realise from the outset that the goal towards which He is beginning to guide you is absolute perfection; and no power in the whole universe, except you yourself, can prevent Him from taking you to that goal. That is what you are in for."

I was far from perfect; I wanted to be less imperfect. But I wished I knew what the improvement plan was going to be. It was unsettling not to know what God was going to do, or how (or when!) he was going to do it. It was like sitting in a room with a door left ajar at my back—a door that I couldn't even close, much less securely lock. Every draft and creak of hinges reminded me I wasn't safe from interference . . .

Interlude 6

At my college in Southern California, all the faculty offices opened directly to the outside of the building, and the weather was so temperate that it was possible to keep the door open nearly all the time. I liked that: students could drop in any time with a question or just to chat. One young man who had taken several of my classes, and who knew I was a Christian, was in the habit of stopping by to say hello every now and again. One day at the end of the fall semester, he dashed in, slightly wild-eyed.

"Professor!"

"Yes?"

"Will you pray for me?"

I was a little startled. "Uh, sure. What for?"

"See, I have this math test next period, and I'm really nervous about it, and I really need to do well, and you know I hate tests, and so, I thought, I really want you to pray for me."

So I stood up and put my hand on his shoulder, and he bowed his head. The incongruity of it struck me; he had one earpiece of his iPod still in, and I could hear the tinny and frenetic strains of rock music. I prayed, asking God's blessing on this young man and his studies, in Jesus' name. We said "Amen", and my student said "Thanks, professor!" and dashed out the door.

I sat back down in my office chair, bemused.

Sometimes I wonder if the acts I do when least prepared will turn out to be the central works God has set out for me to do. Father Doran said to me once, "God keeps me on a need-to-know basis about my future." Me too, Father, me too.

Chapter 22

THE BLADE

Peter took down his gift—the shield with the great red lion on it, and the royal sword. He blew, and rapped them on the floor, to get off the dust. He fitted the shield on his arm and slung the sword by his side. He was afraid at first that it might be rusty and stick to the sheath. But it was not so. With one swift motion he drew it and held it up, shining in the torchlight.

—C. S. Lewis, *Prince Caspian*

My confession of faith was very undramatic. I had been at a high pitch of intense thought and internal struggle, in a process that even carried over into my dreams. I came to a decision, and then ... I didn't do anything right away. I told my coach, and was content to let him tell me what I was supposed to do. (As he did.) I spoke a few words. That was it. I thought that I had arrived at the end of my journey, and in a certain way, I had. Nonetheless, I was left with a nagging feeling that things might not be quite so neatly wrapped up.

I was right.

The sense that I was now on the beginning stages of another and much longer journey came clear on the first day after my profession of faith. We were all still in Las Vegas, and I was fencing in the women's sabre team event.

In this event, three fencers on a team fence relay-style to a total of forty-five points against another team of three fencers; each person rotates in and then out again, fencing once against each of the opposing team members. The person who fences in the very last bout is called the 'anchor', since she is responsible for finishing up the bout, preferably in victory by either holding the lead until forty-five or by coming back from a deficit.

In my first rotation in, I fenced no more than adequately. I needed to do better if we were to win. Then, in the second bout, my performance deteriorated rapidly. It was a domino effect: I lost a point, then got angry with myself for losing the point, which made me tense up and make big, clumsy actions that were even less effective. I knew I was supposed to do better, and I was swiftly approaching the boiling point in self-directed anger.

Apparently, my coach had been telling me "Calm down! Calm down!" from the sidelines during the entire bout, but I was too consumed with anger even to hear him, let alone to pay attention. Finally the bout ended, with me having dropped our team into a deficit. As I walked off the strip my temper snapped and I screamed, loudly, with obscenity. In front of my teammates, my coach, and everyone else watching the team event.

One look at Josh's appalled expression told me all I needed to know: that this was unacceptable behavior. A sickening knot formed in my stomach. I set down my sabre and mask and went off to sit in a corner.

I had one more bout to fence, and as it turned out, I was in the crucial anchor position. Oh, no. I walked back, very quietly, and took my place on the strip. I managed to win the bout and secure the overall win for our team in that round; I was grateful that my ill-mannered display of temper hadn't cost my team too much. In the next round, Josh pulled me from the anchor position; I fenced more or less competently, and we ended up medaling in the event.

I was horribly embarrassed. Clearly, recognizing God as calling me to a higher standard of moral behavior was not the same thing as being able to live up to those standards. Evidently I had an awful lot of work to do, and it looked like it started right here, right now. Although in the past I would have tried to brush off the incident as unimportant, I knew I had to behave differently now. I would have preferred to make light of it; instead I gritted my teeth and apologized to my teammates.

Back at practice the following week, to my surprise I realized that nobody was holding my outburst against me. In retrospect, I would venture to say that if I hadn't been genuinely contrite, I would still have been in trouble with my coach. But I had recognized my fault, been sorry for it, and made amends as best I could, and Josh knew it.

I had resolved that from now on, I wanted to keep my temper always under control; the only problem was, I didn't know how. I needed my coach's help. "Josh, I behaved really badly at the tournament."

"Yes, you did."

(Ouch. But that wasn't a rebuke; it was a statement of fact.)

"I want to learn how to do better."

"Good. Let's work on some ways you can control your temper when you're fencing."

No easy fixes there: but instead, over the next three years, slow progress (and a few setbacks) as Josh helped me figure out how to manage my emotions during a fencing bout, how to be brave and fight for the victory, and how not to be so hard on myself when I made mistakes or fell short of my own expectations for my performance. As a Christian fencer with a Christian coach, I learned to take fencing as a real gift and a source of joy, but not the highest priority in my life. Dealing with injuries and disappointing tournament results provided many opportunities for me to face spiritual weaknesses on a practical level. I began to see connections between what I was learning as a fencer and what I was hearing in church, in Scripture. The disparate, once-fragmented parts of my life were becoming a whole.

Fencing was a discipline that helped me understand what it meant to be made in the image of God. It was also a real-time metaphor for the spiritual life. For most Christians, learning to pick up the "sword of the Spirit" and put on the "helmet of salvation" (Eph 6:17) would have had no personal resonance. But for me, as a fencer, the images communicated something of practical and vital importance: swords and helmets were things to be used, not merely ornamental ways of speaking. I soon discovered that combatting my impatience and my lack of self-control really did require reliance on spiritual weaponry.

As a fencer, I could recognize when I had improved, yet still strive for greater excellence. Becoming a better and better fencer meant continual attention to the details, day in and day out, and learning from those who were more expert than I was. Likewise, with my journey in the Christian faith: it required action (for faith without works is dead) and daily discipline and a willingness to accept the guidance of others.

A few years later, I would retire from the sport, after nearly two decades as a competitive fencer. In that time, I had traveled all over the United States, fenced in Division I events, even competed against women who were on the international team. (I fenced, just once, against an Olympian.

She beat me, but I scored a few touches!) I had made the National Points list. I had a box full of medals.

But I was pushing myself physically beyond my capacity. I was constantly in pain from one or another injury. My opponents were younger, stronger, faster, and, I had to admit, better strategists than I was. I realized that I was not capable of making top ten in a Division I event, and I didn't have the tactical ability to win regional events. I had reached the top of my game, and it was high ... but not as high as I had dreamed.

The last, best lesson I learned from fencing was that there are times and seasons for all things. The end of one chapter of the story is necessary for the beginning of another. If I had continued to compete and had escaped serious injury, in a few years I would have been one of the top contenders in the United States in the forty-plus age category; I would finally have had a good chance at a National title. Even just a few years earlier, I would have imagined that letting go of this long-held dream would be wrenching ... but it wasn't. Fencing had been an important part of my life for many years; I looked back on it with only pleasure and gratitude. Now, though, I sensed that my strength and energy and attention were required for a different kind of battle, and I turned the page with a sense of peace.

When I got ready to move from San Diego to Houston for my new job as an apologist, I did a major purge of my belongings. I gave most of my fencing gear to my alma mater's fencing club, but I was left with an extra sabre. As it happened, St. Michael's by-the-Sea was having its annual all-parish yard sale, so I brought the sabre, along with various other donated items, over to the church. When I got there, I thought to myself, "I bet Father Doran will think it's cool that there's a sword in the yard sale!"

So I picked up the sabre and walked across the church campus. I spotted him coming out of the side door of the church, and said "Hey, Father Doran! Look, I'm donating a sabre!"

He stared at me as if he'd seen a ghost. I was puzzled. What had I said?

Father Doran looked at my sabre. "Seriously, dude, you're donating that sword?"

"Uh ... yeah."

It turns out that just moments before I'd hailed him, Father Doran had been examining a statue of Saint Michael the Archangel that for years had been collecting dust in a storage closet of the church, shoved behind boxes of Christmas decor. It was a dramatic statue, with an athletic Saint Michael about to strike a deathblow with his sword to the monstrous form of Satan beneath his feet ... except that his sword was missing. As Father Doran had stepped out of the church, he'd been thinking: "If only we had a sword that we could put in Saint Michael's hand!"

I disassembled the sabre and we held the blade up next to Saint Michael's grip on the hilt: the sabre blade was just the right proportion; it only needed to be trimmed a bit. A parishioner who was good with tools sawed off the excess and inserted the blade into the hilt. A perfect fit.

And so, in a little parish church in California, there's a statue of Saint Michael the Archangel, leader of the heavenly hosts—sword now in hand—my sword!

Chapter 23

THE WATER

Over went the boat, and [the Mole] found himself struggling in the river.

O my, how cold the water was, and O, how *very* wet it felt! How it sang in his ears as he went down, down, down! How bright and welcome the sun looked as he rose to the surface coughing and spluttering! How black was his despair when he felt himself sinking again! Then a firm paw gripped him by the back of his neck. It was the Rat, and he was evidently laughing ...

—Kenneth Grahame, *The Wind in the Willows*

When I got home from the Las Vegas tournament, I discovered a new challenge, one that couldn't be overcome by reading more books. I had to learn how to follow Christ day by day: to deal with the troubles in my life that had not gone away; to face the flaws in my character; and to participate in this larger life that had somehow opened up before me. I knew that I *was* now a Christian, but I didn't yet know what it *meant*.

Praying was a strange experience. I stumbled over my words, not knowing exactly what to say and keenly aware of how rough and unpolished I sounded.

A few days later, I told Josh that I had begun trying to pray. "I feel like I'm making kind of a muddle of it, though", I admitted.

He reassured me: "God hears even the most awkward prayers."

I continued praying, awkwardly but persistently.

Here I was, in this new country, not exactly lost but not sure of the territory, either. "What do people do when they've decided to be Christians?" I asked Josh.

"Well," he said, "they go to church, and they get baptized."

It was Peter's answer to the crowds when, cut to the heart by his preaching on the day of Pentecost, they asked "What shall we do?" (Acts 2:37).

The prospect of going to church was distinctly unappealing, though it no longer seemed impossible. As for baptism, I had only the vaguest idea of what that might entail, but I feared the worst. It almost certainly involved getting publicly fussed over in front of a large group of strangers; the whole thing would probably be kitschy and embarrassing. I resisted. Surely it was enough for me to have accepted Christ's authority; why did I need to get involved with the Church?

In any case, before I faced the idea of baptism and public worship, I figured that a good starting point would be for me to read the Bible.

Well, good plan. Except that the Bible was rather intimidating. I had read the Gospels, but I had read them as history, looking for facts about Jesus. Had I been asked to analyze the Bible as poetry, I could have tackled the task without a second thought. However, I didn't have the slightest idea how to approach the Bible as a Christian. Even just knowing that it was not just 'Scripture' but 'Holy Scripture', inspired by the God to whom I had committed myself, was more than a little daunting.

Lacking a better plan, I continued from the Gospels into Acts, where I got hopelessly lost among all the shipwrecks and speeches and travels. And then there were all those letters by Paul, who even Peter said was "hard to understand" (2 Pet 3:16)!

Josh probably anticipated (or swiftly noticed) that I was at a loss. "Holly," he said, "you need to start going to church."

"Can I go with you and your family first?" I asked. (Which really meant: "Don't send me out there alone! I'm afraid of those Christians!")

So one Sunday I met Josh and Heidi and their family, and we all went to their church together. I was glad to be part of a family group, even for just a day. I felt safer that way.

It was a distinctly unsatisfying experience. I'd never been to a church service before, but I had visited cathedrals as a tourist; it felt odd to me that a church should look like an auditorium, with stadium seating and a stage for the preacher and the choir. If it weren't for the fact that most of the attendees had brought Bibles, it could have been a concert or public lecture. There was no art, no imagery to remind me of Christ; the songs (whose lyrics were projected on big screens) seemed blandly sentimental. I felt like a spectator at a performance that had nothing to do with me. At least the sermon was informative; I supposed that if this was what 'church' was like, I could learn to live with it.

After we got back from church, Josh took the opportunity to give me a bit of basic Christian instruction. A few weeks earlier, he had given me a copy of the Nicene Creed, explaining that this was a concise statement of what Christians believe. Sitting at his family's kitchen table, we talked over some of the key ideas from the Nicene Creed. Josh introduced the idea of the Trinity to me, and stressed the importance of what the Creed said: that God truly is Father,

Son, and Holy Spirit—three, and yet one—and that Jesus is both fully man and fully God. "I also think the Nicene Creed is beautiful", he said.

I thought so too. It seemed strange that a statement produced by a Church council was so lovely; my experience with documents produced by committees would have suggested otherwise. But the phrases of the Nicene Creed were both precise and poetic, theologically robust and imaginatively resonant:

> I believe in one God,
> the Father almighty,
> maker of heaven and earth,
> of all things visible and invisible.
>
> I believe in one Lord Jesus Christ,
> the only begotten Son of God,
> born of the Father before all ages.
> God from God, Light from Light,
> true God from true God,
> begotten, not made, consubstantial with the Father;
> through him all things were made.
> For us men and for our salvation
> he came down from heaven,
> and by the Holy Spirit was incarnate of the Virgin Mary,
> and became man.
>
> For our sake he was crucified under Pontius Pilate,
> he suffered death and was buried,
> and rose again on the third day
> in accordance with the Scriptures.
> He ascended into heaven
> and is seated at the right hand of the Father.
> He will come again in glory
> to judge the living and the dead
> and his kingdom will have no end.

I believe in the Holy Spirit, the Lord, the giver of life,
who proceeds from the Father and the Son,
who with the Father and the Son is adored and glorified,
who has spoken through the prophets.

I believe in one, holy, catholic and apostolic Church.
I confess one baptism for the forgiveness of sins
and I look forward to the resurrection of the dead
and the life of the world to come. Amen.

Here was a breath of beauty and meaning, like a reviving breeze on a sultry summer's day. If Christianity ever threatened to overawe me with its hugeness, its unendingness, I could always return to this concise and elegant summary of its core.

We talked a little bit about different traditions of worship. My conversion had been to what C. S. Lewis called "mere Christianity", but I could not stay there, reading the Bible in a corner by myself. As Lewis explained:

'Mere' Christianity ... is more like a hall out of which doors open into several rooms. If I can bring anyone into that hall I shall have done what I attempted. But it is in the rooms, not in the hall, that there are fires and chairs and meals ... of course, even in the hall, you must begin trying to obey the rules which are common to the whole house. And above all you must be asking which door is the true one; not which pleases you best by its paint and panelling. In plain language, the question should never be: 'Do I like that kind of service?' but 'Are these doctrines true: Is holiness here?'

I conceded that I needed a home church to attend every Sunday, but I also recognized how out of place I felt at Josh and Heidi's church. I did not know enough to make a good decision on my own, so I asked them to help.

A couple weeks later they sent me a suggestion. I drove over to the church, walked around the grounds and looked at the buildings. It was a weekday, so the campus was deserted; somehow it felt cold and dead. I could not imagine worshiping there. Disappointed, I continued with my other errands.

On the way home, I decided to stop by another church I had seen many times as I drove along the Coast Highway. No one was around, but this place felt peaceful rather than abandoned. There were flower gardens; a statue of Saint Francis, slightly hidden by weeds; a chapel with a wooden cross over the entrance. I felt drawn to this place. I made note of the name and e-mailed Josh when I got home. Was this a good church? He said it was; and so St. Michael's by-the-Sea became my first church home.

After I'd been a month or so at St. Michael's and had met with my priest a couple of times, the subject of baptism came up. "You know, Holly," Father Doran said, "we've got to get you baptized."

"Uh, OK", I said. Surprisingly, it didn't sound scary when he talked about it.

"Let's see ... the next time that we do baptisms is the feast day of Saint Michael and All Angels—that's the first of October. Sound good to you?"

That was just a couple of weeks away. "Sure, I guess", I said. This baptism thing was taking on the definite outlines of reality.

Father Doran explained that I needed a sponsor for my baptism, like a godparent but for adults. It seemed pretty clear to me that Josh was the right person to be my sponsor. "I'll ask my coach, but is it OK that he's not from St. Michael's?" I asked, hesitantly.

"Oh, no problem! He's a good Christian!"

Sunday, October 1, the Feast of Saint Michael and All Angels at our parish, I was nervous, waiting for everyone to arrive at the church. Would they be late? No, here they were, right on time! And dressed up: Josh in a suit and tie, and Heidi in a dress, very formal for Southern California!

I was nervous, talking too much and getting too anxious about all the little details. I wanted to compose myself. "Josh, can we pray together a little bit, before we go into the church?"

"Sure", he said, and we sat down on a bench next to the chapel. The small courtyard, with rosebushes blooming on all sides and a stately stone Celtic cross at one side, formed a tiny oasis of tranquility. Quietly, he thanked God for all that he had done for me, and in me. I remember one image from Josh's prayer: of myself as a branch of a wild tree, about to be grafted onto the good olive tree, from which I would receive life and be able to grow in the faith.

We went into the church and were seated; the bell outside rang; the service began.

Prayer, readings from Scripture, a sermon: and then it was time for my baptism. We all stood up, in full view of the congregation since the reserved pews for the baptismal candidates were up front. Father Doran walked from the sanctuary area to stand in the center aisle, next to my pew

Josh said, quietly but clearly, "I present Holly Elizabeth to receive the sacrament of baptism."

Father Doran turned to me. "Do you desire to be baptized?"

"I do."

Then he asked me the series of questions addressed to candidates for baptism. When we had first discussed baptism, he had given me a copy of the Book of Common Prayer and gone over the section of the baptismal liturgy with me, so I knew exactly what to expect. Even so, I felt the weight of the words as I spoke the answer to each question.

"Do you renounce Satan and all the spiritual forces of wickedness that rebel against God?"

"I renounce them."

"Do you renounce the evil powers of this world which corrupt and destroy the creatures of God?"

"I renounce them."

"Do you renounce all sinful desires that draw you from the love of God?"

"I renounce them."

"Do you turn to Jesus Christ and accept him as your Savior?"

"I do." Such small words to carry such meaning.

"Do you put your whole trust in his grace and love?"

"I do."

"Do you promise to follow and obey him as your Lord?"

"I do."

I did not yet love God, nor grasp that he genuinely loves me. I was incapable of fulfilling any of my baptismal vows on my own power. I spoke the vows myself, unlike the baby who was also being baptized that day, but in reality I was just as weak and helpless as an infant, as dependent on God's grace as the baby on his mother's milk.

The liturgy continued with the Nicene Creed and with prayer; then our little group of candidates and priests and sponsors and friends moved to the entrance of the church, to the baptismal font. I waited nervously while Father Doran blessed the water, and then I leaned over the font, feeling a bit awkward. Father Doran scooped up water in a silver oyster shell and gently poured it over my head, three times: "Holly Elizabeth, I baptize you in the name of the Father, and of the Son, and of the Holy Spirit. Amen." He smiled at me, and gave me a napkin to blot the water off my hair, and I stepped back as he continued to pray, thanking God for this new life of grace.

Turning to me once again, he traced the sign of the cross on my forehead with holy oil and said: "Holly, you are sealed by the Holy Spirit in baptism and marked as Christ's own for ever."

Christ's own for ever ... Your will be done, not mine, Lord.

The rector handed me a candle, lit from the great paschal candle in the church.

"Receive the light of Christ."

I carried the candle back to my seat, blew the flame out as instructed so as not to set fire to the service-sheet or drip wax all over the pew (liturgy has to be practical!), and attended to the rest of the service. When it came to Holy Communion I received the sacrament for the first time, no longer just a prayer of blessing, when I knelt at the altar rail. Now I was a baptized Christian and part of Christ's Body, the Church. How unlikely this all had seemed, even just a few months before!

In the months following my baptism, I discovered something strange and wonderful. I felt that I was being remade, but not into a different person: rather, I was the same 'me' as before, only becoming more fully myself. Something had happened, something real. I began to see, slowly, that this Christian life went beyond understanding theology and learning a new moral code, and that Sunday worship—here, the celebration of the Eucharist—was something more than an opportunity to hear a sermon and Scripture readings.

It was more comfortable for me to focus on developing my faith by studying Scripture and theology and philosophy, but my attention was drawn back again and again to the Cross: to the quiddity of it, to its absurd and scandalous physicality.

G.K. Chesterton says this about the Cross, in his book *Orthodoxy*:

> The cross, though it has at its heart a collision and a contradiction, can extend its four arms for ever without altering its shape. Because it has a paradox in its centre it can grow without changing. The circle returns upon itself and is bound. The cross opens its arms to the four winds; it is a signpost for free travelers.

Whatever it meant to follow Jesus, it certainly meant being broken out of my private, interior world.

Chapter 24

THE MORNING STAR

Far above the Ephel Duath in the West the night-sky was still
dim and pale. There, peeping among the cloud-wrack above
a dark tor high up in the mountains, Sam saw a white star
twinkle for a while. The beauty of it smote his heart.

—J. R. R. Tolkien, *The Lord of the Rings*

On my second trip to England, I went once again to Durham.

Durham Cathedral contains the tomb of the Venerable
Bede, an eighth-century monk who seemed to be interested
in just about everything: he wrote scholarly books on subjects ranging from theology and Scripture to the natural sci-
ences, poetry, and music theory. His *Ecclesiastical History of the
English People* is still used today as the main source of information about early English history; he pioneered the A.D.
dating system; he calculated how the moon influences the
tides. I admired his intellect (and his industry), but perhaps
most of all, I liked that Bede didn't compartmentalize his
faith and his scholarship, or draw a line between 'religious'
and 'nonreligious' subjects.

I woke up early so that I could go to morning prayer.
At that hour, the cathedral was empty of tourists. The sun
slanted through the stained-glass windows high above, dappling the plain gray walls with purple and red and blue. I

157

walked quietly to the west end of the cathedral, to the chapel housing the Venerable Bede's tomb. More than twelve hundred years ago, he had lived, worked, prayed, studied, and written; today, his body in Durham Cathedral is a reminder of the physicality of our faith.

Bede's tomb is a plain stone slab with candles at the four corners; on the wall above it is a quotation from Bede's commentary on Revelation: "Christ is the morning star, who, when the night of this world is past, brings to his saints the promise of the light of life and opens everlasting day."

I knelt and prayed, using Bede's words and thinking of my own writing and work:

> I pray you, good Jesus, that as you have given me the grace to drink in with joy the words of your knowledge, so in your loving kindness you will also grant me to come at length to yourself, the source of all wisdom, to stand for ever before your face. Amen.

I walked back out into the main cathedral and paused in the great open space of the nave, beneath the ribbed vault of the roof high overhead. More than nine hundred years of Christian prayer and worship had been lifted up to God on this site, and the very silence here seemed infused with peace.

To be in Durham Cathedral was to be reminded of the communion of saints, of all those who have loved and served Christ with whatever gifts God gave them, in whatever circumstances they found themselves. Mystic saints and meditative saints, active saints and ascetic saints, bold and meek, simple and scholarly, showing that there are many different ways to love and serve Christ.

I walked through the nave into the quire, the area directly behind the sanctuary where the choir sits, and sat down. I looked up and to the right, and saw the great rose window in the east end of the cathedral, softly glowing with the early light. In the quiet before the service began, the pause between breaths of the cathedral, I felt at peace.

Something more had grown in me, so quietly that I had hardly noticed it until that summer. Even as my faith had deepened, I had become more keenly aware of my own weakness, my distance from Christ. Even as I came to recognize his presence with me, I realized just how faint a glimpse of him this was. I longed for more. I wanted not just to know about Jesus, but to know him.

I didn't know, then, that this longing would also have its fulfillment.

Interlude 7

When I was confirmed as a Catholic, I chose Saint Hilda of Whitby as my patron saint. Why Saint Hilda, a seventh-century abbess? Not surprisingly, a poem was involved.

The Anglo-Saxon poem "Caedmon's Hymn", translated into modern English, runs as follows:

> Now we shall honor the guardian of heaven,
> the might of the architect and His mind's purpose,
> the work of the glory-Father; for He,
> Eternal God, author of all wondrous works,
> first created for the children of men
> heaven as a roof, the holy Creator.
> Then the eternal Lord,
> mankind's guardian, made middle-earth,
> the almighty Ruler shaped for men the soil.

Caedmon, the poet, worked as a cowherd in the abbey community of Whitby, where Hilda oversaw both a women's and a men's monastery. The monks enjoyed singing songs after dinner, but Caedmon, who couldn't sing, would sneak out in embarrassment and go work in the stable instead. On one particular night, Caedmon fell asleep in the stable and had a dream-vision in which an angel told him to sing; immediately Caedmon was able to compose and sing a beautiful song praising the Creator. When he woke up, he not only remembered the verses, but was able to produce more of them. He told his superior, who in turn told the abbess, who then had Caedmon sing (presumably off-key) some of his compositions for her.

His poetry was very good indeed, so much so that Hilda encouraged him to give up his employment as a cowherd to become a monk. She arranged for him to be educated in sacred history, so that he could draw on all the great events of creation and redemption and God's action in ancient Israel and in the Church, to create his poetry. And so he did.

I found myself drawn to both these figures in history. First, the poet Caedmon: he never expected the gift of poetry, yet, having been given it, he worked at it, through study and practice. Perseverance was essential to make use of the talent he had been given. It rang true with my experience of writing both prose and poetry. Also, like Caedmon, I can't sing!

But I was drawn even more to Saint Hilda.

She didn't dismiss the idea of a cowherd-turned-poet, but she also used her judgment, listening to his poetry first to discern whether or not it was worth encouraging. It wasn't enough that Caedmon praised God; Saint Hilda wanted to know whether he was doing it in good poetry and good song. When she realized that he had talent, she helped him develop his gift to the fullest.

As abbess, she was an administrator, responsible for a community of both men and women, overseeing its economic functioning as well as its spiritual health. She was a scholar and educator, an advisor to rulers, and a key figure in the Synod of Whitby, where the English church considered and ultimately accepted the claim of Rome's authority. She was recognized and honored in her own day, and from then on, as a woman leader and a teacher in the Church.

Saint Hilda, pray for me!

Chapter 25

PARADIGM SHIFT

Scientists then often speak of the "scales falling from the eyes" or the "lightning flash" that "inundates" a previously obscure puzzle, enabling its components to be seen in a new way that for the first time permits its solution.... No ordinary sense of the term 'interpretation' fits these flashes of intuition through which a new paradigm is born.

—Thomas Kuhn, *The Structure of Scientific Revolutions*

I've written thus far about events upon which I have some perspective, from seven years' worth to thirty-plus years. Now I arrive at the part of the story that is, of necessity, quite different: my journey into the Catholic Church. All that I can give is a sketched map of territory I've only just begun to explore, an account of experiences whose importance I am still discovering.

What can I say about becoming Catholic?

1. It is by far the best thing I have ever done.
2. It is the most significant event of my life.
3. It will take a lifetime fully to discover what points 1 and 2 mean.

Rather to my surprise, being Catholic has proved to be far more than an ecclesiological or doctrinal commitment. It is, rather, a voyage of discovery involving my whole person:

spiritual, physical, emotional, intellectual. I had thought I understood what it meant to be part of the Body of Christ, what the Eucharist is, what it is to love God and know that I am loved: and yet what I thought I knew turned out to be partial glimpses of something vastly bigger, stranger, richer, deeper than I had ever guessed.

How did I get here?

G. K. Chesterton said it well: "The difficulty of explaining 'why I am a Catholic' is that there are ten thousand reasons all amounting to one reason: that Catholicism is true." Indeed.

Yet to talk about the journey as if it were only, or even primarily, a weighing of the evidence, a consideration of the doctrinal and Scriptural and historical issues, or a comparison of the merits of the Catholic Church versus the Episcopal Church or what-have-you as a new church home, would be to miss the essence of what happened. It would be like trying to explain falling in love by enumerating the outstanding qualities of the beloved: the list will contain things that seem utterly irrelevant to a third party, and will be both completely true and completely useless.

Writing about becoming Catholic is something like my writing about England. The things that are the easiest to talk about are seldom the most important. I could show a photo of Big Ben in London and be sure of an appreciative response, but that response will be to something other than what I really love, like giving someone a cup of hot chocolate in the hopes that they'll appreciate the merits of good coffee.

I could describe Oxford: the Eagle & Child pub; the sunlight on a summer afternoon glowing along the stonework across the street from Blackfriars; the clusters of tiny purple-petaled flowers that grow in crevices on stone walls; the changing sky reflected in the water of the canal in all weathers; the dark-glossy-green holly trees in the wooded hills east of the city; or the layers of history, century upon century, preserved in street names and half-hidden monuments. But none of this would explain the very thing that matters most.

How can I show you the way an intuited sense of connection unfolded into the unexpected recognition that this is 'home'?

I can only hope to help you catch a glimpse for yourself.

Six and a half years after my baptism into the Body of Christ, I was entering a new stage in my life. I had accepted an offer to lead a brand-new apologetics program in Houston, Texas. It was a big decision, though in the end not a complicated one. This was my dream job, in more ways than one: I hadn't even applied for it, but had been recruited. I would miss my old church, but I knew that there were several large, dynamic Anglican churches in Houston, and I fully anticipated joining one of them when I arrived.

At the end of that spring semester, I said goodbye to my friends in California and got a lovely send-off from St. Michael's by-the-Sea. I sold my house, put all my worldly goods in storage, and, in early June, hopped on a plane to spend the summer in England. When I returned in August, I would make the trip from San Diego to Houston, to a new apartment, a new job, and a new church home.

The summer in Oxford was a deliberate drawing of breath, an in-between place for an in-between time.

I found myself at loose ends, though. Something had become unsettled. Stepping out of my comfortable routine, saying goodbye to a familiar pattern of life, had forced me to step back and consider the shape of my commitment to Christ and his Kingdom.

I was too Catholic-minded to feel entirely at home in the Evangelical world, though that was the context for most of my apologetics ministry, but I was too theologically conservative to feel entirely at home in the Anglican world, either.

As I thought about where I would attend church in the fall, I became uncomfortably aware that I was preparing to make accommodations ... deciding which issues were not quite as irksome to my conscience as others. Then, to my dismay, I realized that I had already been making accommodations, without admitting it.

I had been able to ignore the question of women's ordination, despite being convinced of the Scriptural and theological basis for a male priesthood, only because there had been no women clergy at St. Michael's. I had become convinced of the need to speak out more clearly and strongly on issues of sexual ethics—against abortion; against the contraceptive culture that broke the link between sex and new life, and promoted sex as merely a recreational activity; and in support of traditional marriage—but I had remained largely silent, knowing that some or all of these positions were controversial for many of my fellow Christians.

Could I just keep on as I was? 'Mere Christianity' was an excellent framework for collaboration and cooperation with my fellow Christians as an academic and an apologist, but was it strong enough to carry the whole weight of my life of faith?

Mentally, I put the question back on the shelf. Time enough to deal with that later.

Early in the summer, I was talking with an Anglican friend, the conversation variously touching on his writing projects and the current goings-on in the Church of England, when he told me of his intention to become a Catholic.

I was startled—and my response was immediate, honest, and completely unpremeditated: "I'm headed toward Rome, too."

Say *what*?

I'd put into words something that I knew was true, even as I said it, but that I had not until that very moment consciously acknowledged. It was a divine set-up. If I had been talking to a colleague or acquaintance, I would have said something encouraging without committing myself. If I'd had some forewarning about the turn the conversation would take, I might have second-guessed my words. But in that moment, I wasn't thinking about myself, only about my friend's announcement. And then, having actually said these words to him out loud, I could not pretend that this was just a passing thought. What other circumstances could have startled me into speaking so truthfully, or so vividly shown me where I stood?

As C. S. Lewis noted, "God, is, if I may say it, very unscrupulous."

What was most unnerving was the realization that I wasn't looking so much at a decision to be *made*, but at one already made that I needed to recognize and act on.

Lewis had described 'mere Christianity' as a hallway from which led off other rooms: Methodist, Baptist, Catholic, Lutheran, and so on. Having entered the house, you couldn't linger forever in the hall; you had to pick a room to live in, with its own furniture and ways of doing things, but there was a fundamental equality to the different rooms.

I liked the idea. It sounded attractively humble, in contrast to the Catholic claim that their church is the true Church with decisive authority. I knew that Catholics would consider me, a non-Catholic, to be a Christian, but one of the 'separated brethren'. That's a two-edged statement. On the one hand, it affirms the shared Christianness of all baptized believers. But on the other hand, it presumes a position of judgment by the Catholic Church.

Did the Catholic Church hold that I, as a faithful Christian in the Anglican tradition, had an inadequate or incomplete faith? (Yes.) Who did the Church think it was, to make claims like that? Arrogance—pure arrogance. How could anyone take this seriously?

Except I knew perfectly well, as an apologist, that any absolute truth-claim is provocative. Claims like this are either true or false. If one believes that the claim is true, then it would be false humility to pretend otherwise. "Jesus is the only way of salvation" is an incredibly arrogant statement, but it happens to be true.

I liked the image of Catholicism as one more room in the large Christian house. I could enjoy their contribution to the common life of the house, borrow their furniture, copy their décor, without feeling obligated to consider their call to total commitment.

But the picture that Catholics had of their Church was not nearly so contained, so safe and tame. That summer I read G. K. Chesterton's book *The Catholic Church and Conversion*, a book that had been on my to-read list for quite some time. He describes the conventional view of the different denominations with a vivid image of the churches as exhibits set up side by side in the Crystal Palace exhibition hall:

> Here stood all the religions in a row—the churches or sects or whatever we called them; and towards the end of the row there was a particularly dingy and dismal one, with a pointed roof half fallen in and pointed windows most broken with stones by passers-by; and we were told that this particular exhibit was the Roman Catholic Church.... Now conversion consists very largely, on its intellectual side, in the discovery that all that picture of equal creeds inside an indifferent cosmos is quite false. It is not a question of comparing the merits and defects of the Quaker meeting-house set beside the Catholic cathedral. It is the Quaker meeting-house that is inside the Catholic cathedral; it is the Catholic cathedral that covers everything like the vault of the Crystal Palace; and it is when we look up at the vast distant dome covering all the exhibits that we trace the Gothic roof and the pointed windows.

One day I was walking through Headington Hill Park, delighting in the grass spangled with tiny daisies, looking up and seeing the sunlight glowing through the leaves overhead, a canopy of jewel-bright young-spring green mingled with darker-summer green, and blue sky showing in moving glimpses through the leaves.

I had a sudden shift of perspective: as if the interlacing branches of the trees overhead were the arches of a great cathedral, as if the green and blue and white came from the light shining through a stained-glass window. It seemed an image of the Church: old as the ground under my feet, young as the leaves overhead, infinitely larger on the inside than it seemed from outside.

I hadn't learned anything new about Catholicism; rather, I had experienced a paradigm shift. In the days that followed, I realized that I was now looking at the world as a Catholic, and seeing that the totality of my experience, knowledge, and understanding made sense here; were part of a complete and greater whole that extended deeper and higher than I could guess.

I had noticed the great patient quiet presence of the Church.

What was I going to do about it?

Chapter 26

MAGNIFICAT

Crown Him the virgin's Son, the God incarnate born,
Whose arm those crimson trophies won which now His
    brow adorn;
Fruit of the mystic rose, as of that rose the stem;
The root whence mercy ever flows, the Babe of Bethlehem.

—Matthew Bridges, "Crown Him with Many Crowns"

In retrospect, I can see that I'd been moving steadily Rome-ward for more than three years.

I had earned a second master's degree in Christian apologetics at a Protestant university. I didn't start with any serious theological differences from my classmates and professors, and hadn't even considered most of the theological issues that divided Protestants and Catholics (and Protestants among themselves). St. Michael's by-the-Sea was an Anglican church, though, and that set me apart. I wanted to know, why did Anglicans profess what we did, and was it true? And if I was going to compare Anglican teaching with Evangelical Protestant teaching, why not be comprehensive? I got into the habit of looking at what the Orthodox and the Catholics had to say about everything we studied, as well.

Time and again, I came to the conclusion that Catholic doctrine and practice made a lot of sense.

A consistent, workable hermeneutic of Scripture. Ecclesiology that held 'the Body of Christ' as a robust reality both spiritually and visibly. The dignity of the human person, made in the image of God. A solid pro-life, pro-marriage, pro-family ethic. An approach to discipleship, vocation, and worship that included the aesthetic, intellectual, physical, and social dimensions of human life.

Still, I felt comfortable in Anglicanism, which had, as I saw it, all the richness of Catholic tradition and history, combined with a willingness to leave many matters of faith up to the individual conscience. Anglicans, for instance, take the view about confession that 'all can; some should; none must', and church attendance on Sundays is considered a very good thing, but not an obligation. I had begun to realize that the Eucharist was at the heart of my devotional life, but as an Anglican, I didn't have to commit to the doctrine of transubstantiation to explain why it wasn't just a memorial.

The 'big tent' of Anglicanism, with its beautiful Book of Common Prayer, seemed to make room for both Protestant-minded and Catholic-minded folks; it seemed to get all the benefits of Catholic tradition while avoiding the parts that I didn't like.

I was particularly drawn to the Oxford Movement, a nineteenth-century renewal movement within the Anglican church that had produced powerful writing and preaching, and a revival of many of the practices of the early Church. Of course, there was the inconvenient fact that many of the people involved with the Oxford Movement had kept moving all the way to Rome, like John Henry Newman and my particular hero, Gerard Manley Hopkins.

And there was the inconvenient fact that my conscience was well on its way to Rome before I was.

I enjoyed my job as a college English professor, I was good at it, and I knew that I was doing a service by being a Christian in a secular educational environment. Nonetheless, I felt increasingly called to serve the Church more directly.

Then it seemed I'd found the perfect job: teaching in a Great Books program at a solid Christian university in California. I was enthusiastic about the mission of the program and they were excited about my apologetics work; the director of the program encouraged me to apply; it looked like the perfect fit. I could affirm all parts of the university's statement of faith, but I did wonder whether a Protestant university would welcome a high church Anglican. I talked with several members of the hiring committee about that specific question, and got positive replies.

I was excited. An excellent school, a dynamic program, a great location ... I wouldn't even have to sell my house. I worked hard on my application, sent it in, waited, prayed.

Then I got an e-mail from the hiring committee.

Would I please clarify: Did I consider the Anglican church to be a Protestant church?

I knew very well what I was being asked ... and what answer would get me the job.

I could have replied that I was a member of the Protestant Episcopal Church of the United States, even though my particular church had more of an Anglo-Catholic flavor. That would have been reassuring to the committee and also true, in the literal sense of the words; but I didn't write it. Instead I wrote about the Anglican Church as a big tent, pointing out that the Anglican church broke with Rome; I noted that I was not a Roman Catholic. All true.

But there is such a thing as a lie by omission and, uncomfortably aware of that fact, I added that I considered myself an "evangelical reformed catholic". In my mind I capitalized the C, but I was still mincing my words to get the job, so I kept it small-c.

Even that wasn't the whole truth.

I added one more sentence: that I was "definitely not a Protestant".

I closed with the usual polite noises about being glad to be in dialogue, etc., but I knew that if I hit 'send' on this e-mail as I'd written it, I would lose the job.

If I hit 'send' I would be giving up an ideal job, a foundation for my future ministry in apologetics, great connections, exciting work to do for the Kingdom.

And for what? I wasn't Roman Catholic. I wasn't planning or even thinking about going over to Rome. What a waste of a God-given opportunity!

I hit 'send'.

Oddly enough, even after having lost a job over being too Catholic, I was emphatic in saying that I was not *Roman* Catholic. No, definitely not! I was an Anglo-Catholic or an evangelical reformed Catholic. I knew the four marks of the Church (one, holy, catholic, apostolic), and I accepted the last three, but I had reservations about the first. Why need there be just 'one' Catholic church? Why be so narrow, so single-minded? It would commit me to things I was still unsure about.

And anyway, I might agree with Catholics on lots of things, but their dogma and devotional practice related to Mary was an obstacle that I could not get past.

Not that I had tried to find out what the reasoning was for things like the Immaculate Conception or the Assumption. Mary made me uncomfortable. I preferred to keep her safely on the sidelines, and considered that in doing so I was honoring Jesus by keeping him front and center.

Annoyingly, she kept turning up anyway.

Several years prior, I had learned that there was such a thing as the 'Anglican Rosary' (an invention of the 1980s, as it happens) and, for a spiritual formation class, decided to do a research paper on it. This led me to learning about the Catholic Rosary, and discovering that Catholics had quite sensible, Biblically grounded responses to Protestant objections to Marian devotions. Still, I just couldn't bring myself to say the 'Hail Mary'. Never mind that the words came from Scripture.

Then there was Evening Prayer, which I read on Tuesday nights at St. Michael's by-the-Sea. Usually I was alone in the chapel, but I diligently read the whole service from the Book of Common Prayer even if nobody joined me. Evening Prayer has a set structure in which the Scripture readings for the day are each followed by a canticle, an excerpt from Scripture in poetic form. One of the canticles is called the Magnificat, after the opening words in Latin of the Song of Mary: "My soul magnifies the Lord, and my spirit rejoices in God my Savior."

The Book of Common Prayer's translation is stately and beautiful:

My soul doth magnify the Lord, and my spirit hath rejoiced in God my Saviour.
For he hath regarded the lowliness of his handmaiden.
For behold, from henceforth all generations shall call me blessed.
For he that is mighty hath magnified me, and holy is his Name.
And his mercy is on them that fear him throughout all generations.
He hath shewed strength with his arm; he hath scattered the proud in the imagination of their hearts.
He hath put down the mighty from their seat, and hath exalted the humble and meek.

He hath filled the hungry with good things, and the rich he
hath sent empty away.

He remembering his mercy hath holpen his servant Israel,
as he promised to our forefathers, Abraham and his seed
for ever.

I was uncomfortable reading the Magnificat. I hesitated over
it. One day, when the Scripture reading was especially long,
I skipped it for the sake of time. Then I started skipping it
every time, excusing myself by saying that it was okay for me
to condense the service a bit if nobody was there.

Then one day Father Doran dropped in for prayer and
called me on it. "Hey, you forgot the Magnificat. Don't get
sloppy just because you're reading by yourself."

The thing was, I wasn't being careless, or rushed. I knew
exactly why I was skipping the Magnificat.

I was afraid of saying Mary's words after her: as if to repeat
her words of praise would also be to repeat her words at the
Annunciation: "Behold, I am the servant of the Lord; let it
be to me according to your word" (Lk 1:38). I was afraid of
entering into her total, radical obedience.

Get over it, I told myself, and started properly including
the Magnificat in Evening Prayer again. Even if I gave a nod
every week toward Mary, I could safely ignore her the rest
of the time.

Yet any time I opened up a book of medieval art, or
walked into the Renaissance galleries in a museum, I was
confronted with Mary. Icons and devotional art, over and
over again, showed Mary, and not just in Nativity scenes. She
was the Queen of Heaven, the Mother of Sorrows, the Mystical Rose. Somehow for centuries the Church had found
in Mary not a distraction from Jesus, but a pointer toward
him, a way of learning to love him, a model of obedience
and piety.

In studying apologetics, I spent a lot of time learning to defend the historical reality of the bodily Resurrection of Jesus, which led me to think deeply on the importance of the Incarnation. Jesus' body was not just a convenient suit of fleshy clothes to walk around and preach in. His Resurrection is no gnostic salvation of the spirit alone, but the first-fruits of the full, glorious resurrection of each one of us, body and soul. The Incarnation meant, too, that what people do with their bodies matters; that when Jesus talks about marriage bringing man and woman together to become 'one flesh' he is telling us that there is a sacramental reality to the union in its physical as well as emotional dimension; and that the Body of Christ, the Church, was something more than a convenient metaphor, more than a merely invisible, purely spiritual organization. The Incarnation was at the heart of the gospel.

And so I could not help but recognize the truth of what the Church had taught for so long: if Jesus is fully human and also fully God, then his mother Mary is the Mother of the Second Person of the Trinity; she is the Mother of God, the God-bearer, *Theotokos*. Immaculately conceived so as to be able to give to her Son her own flesh unstained by original sin, she is the second Eve, as Jesus is the second Adam.

How could I deny that Mary would have a special bond with her Son who is also her Savior, whom she carried in her womb, whom she nursed, whose dead body she cradled in her arms? More importantly, how could I claim that Jesus, who is the perfect man in every respect, would not obey the Commandment to honor his parents? That he honored his Father, God, was obvious. And now I began to see that he honored his Mother, by giving her a unique status, "blessed among women".

The problem wasn't having too high a view of Mary. It was that I had too low a view of Jesus.

All this went through my mind, that summer in Oxford, as I wrestled with the implications of my turn toward Rome.

I went to Addison's Walk, the path around the Magdalen College meadows where, famously, C. S. Lewis had had the conversation with J. R. R. Tolkien and Hugo Dyson that led him finally to become a Christian. For a long time I paced beside the river, confronting my fear and hesitation.

Haltingly, half-embarrassed, I asked Mary to pray for me.

I'd crossed a Rubicon, but had still not crossed the Tiber.

Chapter 27

COMING HOME

At last they rode over the downs and took the East Road, and then Merry and Pippin rode on to Buckland; and already they were singing again as they went. But Sam turned to Bywater, and so came back up the Hill, as day was ending once more. And he went on, and there was yellow light, and fire within; and the evening meal was ready, and he was expected. And Rose drew him in, and set him in his chair, and put little Elanor upon his lap.

He drew a deep breath. 'Well, I'm back,' he said.

—J.R.R. Tolkien, *The Lord of the Rings*

Oxford is a city whose voice is bells, in churches and college chapels, from great Tom at Christ Church to the noble ring at Magdalen, from Betjeman's "intolerably sad" bells of St Giles to the welcome chiming-bell at Blackfriars. Their sound always felt magical to me, a pure loveliness hinting at something just out of reach.

From reading Dorothy Sayers' novel *The Nine Tailors*, I knew that there was a particular kind of bell-ringing in England called 'change-ringing'; it sounded complicated and intriguing, and I thought it would be interesting to hear it someday.

Then I learned that one of my friends had been a change-ringer, so I asked him to explain it to me. Unlike simple pealing or playing a tune, change-ringing means sounding the bells so as to provide different permutations of the sequence of notes. And, he added, Oxford was famous for its change-ringing: in fact, it was certain that I'd heard it many times and simply not known what it was.

A few days later, as I was walking across town, I heard the bells of St Mary Magdalen. I stopped to listen.

And just like that, the notes fell into place: I could hear the changes. What had been previously an undifferentiated mass of notes—each one lovely but unrelated to the others—crystallized into a pattern. I was transfixed. I sat for half an hour on a sun-warmed stone tomb in nearby St Giles' churchyard, letting the joyous cascading sound wash over me, feeling simultaneously an ache of loss as each note fell away, and a lifting of the heart as, like water, the notes carried on and carried me with them.

I could not go back to hearing the bells as something without a pattern, without meaning.

That summer in Oxford, unsettled by the shift in my perspective, I sought clarity and guidance in the Bible—and found that I understood what I read in a new light; I could no longer fail to see the way it all fit together.

I saw afresh the scandal of the Cross, and how shocking, how dangerous Jesus' words are. "Truly, truly, I say to you, unless you eat the flesh of the Son of Man and drink his blood, you have no life in you" (Jn 6:53). If that was merely a colorful description of a memorial meal, Jesus didn't bother to clarify for those of his disciples who cried, "This is a hard saying; who can listen to it?" (Jn 6:60) and left in disgust. How much nicer and neater to think of the Eucharist as a symbol! But I had become convinced, from Church history, from theology, and from my own experience in worship, that our Lord meant precisely what he said, strange and unsettling as it was to think that the bread and the wine are his flesh, his blood.

Jesus had hard words on many things: on sin, on hell, on the nature of marriage, on the radical commitment necessary to follow him. What if the authority of the Church was one of those hard things? I could not pick and choose.

And as I reread the Gospels, I saw Peter, as if for the first time.

"You are the Christ", Peter said; and Jesus responded, "And I tell you, you are Peter, and on this rock I will build my Church" (Mt 16:16, 18). I knew, as a literary scholar and poet, that the purpose of wordplay is to underscore a point. Jesus' pun on Peter / Petras has its most robust meaning if "this rock" refers to Peter himself, not his confession of faith.

And what of Peter's authority? Jesus spoke directly to him—not to all the apostles, not in a general sermon— when he said, "I will give you the keys of the kingdom of heaven, and whatever you bind on earth shall be bound in heaven, and whatever you loose on earth shall be loosed in heaven" (Mt 16:19). I was uncomfortably aware that I had preferred the Protestant interpretation of this passage precisely because it presupposed that Jesus could not have given this kind of authority to Peter and his successors.

I brought up the question of authority with a friend, sitting in a little café on a quiet side street in Oxford. He pointed out that there was more to consider. Jesus says to Peter, "I have prayed for you that your faith may not fail. And when you have turned again, strengthen your brothers" (Lk 22:32). One can assume that Jesus' prayer will be answered. But immediately after this, Peter denies Jesus three times, as Jesus had said he would. Peter's faith certainly failed. What, then, could Jesus have prayed for?

It is after Peter has "turned again" that his faith will not fail. It is in that role, as the foremost of the apostles, that he will strengthen his brethren: leading them, the first to serve as the head of the Church Universal. Suddenly I realized that, after the Resurrection, Jesus addresses Peter individually, not the disciples as a group the way he does with the great commission (Mt 28:16–20). What if it meant more than I thought, that Jesus not only gave Peter the keys of the kingdom, but also commissioned him to "tend my sheep"? (Jn 21:16).

Once I let go of my determination *not* to see Peter as having received special authority, I saw more and more in Acts that I'd skipped over before: Peter in a new role of authority among the apostles ("Peter and the eleven", Acts 2:14), the one who pronounced judgment on Ananias and Sapphira (Acts 5), the recipient of the revelation that the Gospel was to be brought to the Gentiles (Acts 10), the leader of the newly born Church. Not without faults as a person—Paul once had to oppose him to his face and correct his behavior (Gal 2:11)—but unfailing as the first guardian of the faith that had been delivered to the saints.

The question of authority ran deeper. I had turned to Scripture to guide me on that very issue ... and realized it was the Church, guided by the Spirit, that had determined the canon of Scripture—the Church that was already in existence.

Jesus sent the Holy Spirit to guide us into all truth. Yet the evidence of history is that the Spirit does not guide every individual Christian into a full knowledge of the truth—nor even every devout, intelligent, or well-educated Christian. There are any number of issues on which there must be a right answer, yet Christians disagree: What happens in baptism? What is the age of the earth?

It can't even be that the Spirit inspired the writers of Holy Scripture and left it at that, because devout, intelligent, well-educated Christians differ on the interpretation of Scripture, and even on what constitutes a 'plain reading'. What does the word 'day' mean in Genesis? Is 'this is my body' a metaphor? Like the Ethiopian eunuch in Acts 8, I found myself asking, "How can I understand what I read, unless someone explains it to me?"

The Gospels and Epistles were written in the lifetime of the apostles, but they were written for the Church that already existed, for Christians who were already gathering in worship and being taught by the apostles. Jesus didn't give us a book; he gave us himself, in the Eucharist, and when he sent his Spirit at Pentecost, he gave us the Church. It seemed strange that Jesus would speak so strongly about his Church as to declare that "the gates of Hell shall not prevail against it" (Mt 16:18) if its unity and its truth of doctrine were dependent on flawed, incomplete human understanding. If Scripture was inspired and authoritative, as I believed it was, wouldn't God also provide for its right interpretation? It made sense that an infallible Magisterium, guided by the Holy Spirit, would develop to preserve, transmit, and teach the fullness of "the faith that was once for all delivered to the saints" (Jude 1:3).

And if the Church was something more than a collection of people choosing to worship together—if it really is the Body of Christ—then it remains so, even if some members of the Body choose to separate from it; its authority remains despite the weakness and sinfulness of the individual members entrusted with that authority. The Church is a living and supernatural reality, "the pillar and foundation of truth" (1 Tim 3:15).

I could spend years more studying Catholic doctrine, coming to my own decision on every point, but I realized that if I did, I would be choosing to remain outside the one Church not out of real doubt, but from my own desire to be self-sufficient, in control. Both reason and imagination pointed me in one direction, toward the Catholic Church. The question was not of intellectual assent on every single point, but of obedience. I knew, now, that I had wanted to keep some small part of myself reserved from the total self-surrender to which Christ called me. I wanted to be able to say, I obey the Church in this, or that, because I agree with the Church's teaching on this, or that ... to hold my own judgment as the deciding factor.

Could I step out from behind the shelter of those last remnants of my private fortifications? Would I finally and completely lay down my arms?

That fall, in Houston, I was received into the Catholic Church.

After the intensity of the summer, when I made my decision to cross the Tiber among the dreaming spires of Oxford, I didn't know quite what to expect when I got to Houston. I was braced for big changes ... and nothing much happened. I did lose a book contract that I had with a Protestant publisher, but, happily, my new colleagues at Houston Baptist University and my Evangelical friends took my conversion entirely in stride.

Slowly, I realized that now I was on a different kind of journey. I was home, yes—but after the excitement of arrival, after the suitcases are unpacked, being 'home' takes its shape in the ordinary details of day-to-day life: grocery shopping, laundry, answering e-mail, choosing what to read, or wear, or have for dinner.

As an Anglican, being able to pick and choose my devotional practices, to customize the expression of my faith, had made it far too easy for me to make my faith primarily about my own personal preferences. Now I realized that I needed to enter into the life and tradition of the Church: to learn how to be an ordinary Catholic, in the details.

When I knew that I was going to become a Catholic, I went to Catholic Mass in Oxford with my friends there. Then, in Houston, I began to keep the Friday fast, to go regularly to confession, and to attend daily Mass. For the first time, I encountered the fullness of grace in the Eucharist: it was a veil being drawn aside; a sharp breeze blowing away a muffling haze; the Beloved fully present and touching me, not just his voice heard in the same room. I discovered that sacramental grace impacts every part of the self—body, mind, emotions—and enters into every part of daily life.

What will this journey look like? An ordinary Catholic life ... and yet, I know from the lives of the saints, from the Oxford martyrs, from my Catholic friends, that an ordinary Catholic life is, paradoxically, quite extraordinary.

It would be so very easy and appealing to intellectualize my faith. God gave me my intellectual gifts and my vocation as a teacher and writer; that's in no doubt. But the temptation is to make the focus of my faith be my understanding of Christ, and not Christ himself. It's tempting to individualize my faith, make it 'my own', rather than seeking to enter into the faith of the Church.

I am reminded of Jesus' words: "Truly, I say to you, unless you turn and become like children, you will never enter the kingdom of heaven. Whoever humbles himself like this child, he is the greatest in the kingdom of heaven" (Mt 18:3–4, RSV-2CE).

Part of learning to be childlike has been rediscovering how to imitate others. At first I struggled, discovering a subtle pride in 'doing things my way'. But Saint Paul told the Corinthians to imitate him, as he imitates Christ; if I see that a friend whom I trust and respect does things a certain way, why not follow suit?

At Mass, to genuflect before receiving the Host and the chalice; to observe, as much as possible, a genuine day of rest on Sunday; to pray the Rosary: these are all things that have been a real help to me as I learn how to be a Catholic, and these are all things that I have copied from my friends.

Being childlike also means, I think, being fully present in the experience of worship, not standing aside analyzing it or, God help me, critiquing it. At the Mass, I know the theology that undergirds the doctrine of transubstantiation; it's part of what drew me to become a Catholic. My understanding of the philosophical terms 'substance' and 'accidents', and my knowledge of how the Eucharist has been viewed throughout Church history ... these things are good, but not central. As C. S. Lewis wrote, wisely, "The command, after all, was *Take, eat*: not *Take, understand*."

Our Lord calls us to be "like little children": not childish in understanding, but childlike in trusting love. I feel this most keenly in the moment of receiving the Host on the tongue: mouth open, like a little bird. At first, it made me feel awkward, abashed, not like an adult. This was all to the good. I am reminded that it is not by being a confident academic, a defender of the faith, that I somehow merit this grace; rather, I am a child coming to her Father, secure in the knowledge that she is loved completely.

I may have let down my guard fully on entering the Church, but now I must learn to keep it down, resisting the subtle pull of pride; to surrender the fierce territorial claim that my old self repeatedly makes; to become, day by day, in new ways I can't even yet imagine, ever more open to adventure, to simplicity—and to joy.

Acknowledgments

Many people had a hand in bringing this book to be.

I would like to start by thanking Father Joseph Fessio and Mark Brumley, at Ignatius Press, for taking me on as an author, and Joseph Pearce, for helping make it happen. I could not be more delighted to have my book published by this fine press.

John Mark Reynolds has encouraged my work for years, and given me the opportunity to be part of the HBU apologetics team, going boldly where no apologists have gone before. Let me take this opportunity to say 'thank you' for that, as well as for writing the introduction to this book. I would also like to express my appreciation of President Robert Sloan and all my colleagues at Houston Baptist University.

A hearty thank-you goes to all the bloggers, conference organizers, radio shows, and churches who have shared my work and invited me to tell my story over the past few years, and to all the readers of the first edition of *Not God's Type*.

I am grateful for the prayer and support of my friends, too many to name, but especially: Mario Alejandre, Kevin Belmonte, Ashley Canter, Patrick Gardella, Ken Mann, and Melissa Travis.

Special thanks go to three of my friends.

Malcolm Guite inspired me to turn my academic work toward imaginative apologetics, and encouraged me to develop more fully the story of how literature played a role in my coming to faith.

Kelly Belmonte's writerly support has been invaluable. Also, the 'Caedmon and Hilda' section of this book first appeared, in a slightly different form, on Kelly's excellent blog *All Nine Muses*.

My warmest thanks go to Michael Ward, author of *Planet Narnia*, for his steadfast support on the journey, for his encouragement of my writing, and for his insightful comments and suggestions on the draft of the manuscript. This book is vastly better for his influence.

Oxford, England
The Feast of the Annunciation, March 25, 2014

"I stand in Minas Anor, the Tower of the Sun," [Eowyn] said; "and behold! the Shadow has departed! I will be a shieldmaiden no longer, nor vie with the great Riders, nor take joy only in the songs of slaying. I will be a healer, and love all things that grow and are not barren."

—J. R. R. Tolkien, *The Lord of the Rings*